Library Performance and Service Competition: Developing strategic responses

LARRY NASH WHITE

Chandos Publishing

Oxford · England

Chandos Publishing (Oxford) Limited
TBAC Business Centre
Avenue 4
Station Lane
Witney
Oxford OX28 4BN
UK
Tel: +44 (0) 1993 848726 Fax: +44 (0) 1865 884448
Email: info@chandospublishing.com
www.chandospublishing.com

First published in Great Britain in 2008

ISBN:
978 1 84334 314 1 (paperback)
978 1 84334 315 8 (hardback)
1 84334 314 2 (paperback)
1 84334 315 0 (hardback)

Typeset by Domex e-Data Pvt. Ltd.
Printed in the UK and USA.

Library Performance and Service Competition

CHANDOS
INFORMATION PROFESSIONAL SERIES

Series Editor: Ruth Rikowski
(email: Rikowskigr@aol.com)

Chandos' new series of books are aimed at the busy information professional. They have been specially commissioned to provide the reader with an authoritative view of current thinking. They are designed to provide easy-to-read and (most importantly) practical coverage of topics that are of interest to librarians and other information professionals. If you would like a full listing of current and forthcoming titles, please visit our web site **www.chandospublishing.com** or contact Hannah Grace-Williams on email info@chandospublishing.com or telephone number +44 (0) 1993 848726.

New authors: we are always pleased to receive ideas for new titles; if you would like to write a book for Chandos, please contact Dr Glyn Jones on email gjones@chandospublishing.com or telephone number +44 (0) 1993 848726.

Bulk orders: some organisations buy a number of copies of our books. If you are interested in doing this, we would be pleased to discuss a discount. Please contact Hannah Grace-Williams on email info@chandospublishing.com or telephone number +44 (0) 1993 848726.

I would like to dedicate this work to Thomas L. Nash and Les White, and most importantly my wife Emily Blankenship, for all of their contributions to my understanding, knowledge and success in my personal and professional life.

Contents

List of figures and tables

Figures

Tables

About the author

Larry Nash White (MLS, PhD) is an assistant professor and the Master of Library Science program director in the Department of Library Science and Instructional Technology at East Carolina University and is a recipient of a *Library Journal* '2007 Movers and Shakers Award' for his innovative approaches to library management and education. Dr White is an internationally invited speaker and presenter on library performance assessment, strategy and competition for library and information services. He has published in the areas of current issues and future trends in library performance assessment, competition for library and information services and the financial management of libraries. He has previous experience as an administrator in retail management and in many administrative roles within public and academic libraries.

Dr White is a two-time graduate of Florida State University (MLS, PhD), is married to an incredible reference librarian named Emily, enjoys music and genealogy, and lives in Greenville, North Carolina, with his three dogs.

The author can be contacted via the publisher or at *whitel@ecu.edu*.

Acknowledgements

I would like first to acknowledge the constructive feedback and patience of my editorial support, Dr Glyn Jones and Cherry Ekins, in the creation of this work. Next I would like to acknowledge the patient support of my wife Emily, who listened, debated and sacrificed to allow me to complete this book. Lastly, I would like to acknowledge the valued welcome and support from my colleagues within the Library Science and Instructional Technology Department and the College of Education at East Carolina University, who have helped me acclimatize and be successful in my new home in Greenville, North Carolina.

List of acronyms

AAA	access, accountability and alignment
ALA	American Library Association
BSC	balanced scorecard
CI	competitive intelligence
CILIP	Chartered Institute of Library and Information Professionals
IFLA	International Federation of Library Associations
IMLS	Institute for Museum and Library Services
ODK	orphaned data and knowledge
PM	performance measurement
ROA	return on assets
ROI	return on investment
TCO	total cost of ownership
TQC	total quality control
TQM	total quality management

How long have we been counting things? An overview of library service performance assessment

Assessing the performance of libraries has its roots in the performance assessment of business. Understanding the history and development of business performance assessment provides a required backdrop to the development of library performance assessment, as many of the library's current assessment processes and metrics are based on business assessment processes and metrics.

Evaluating business organizations was fairly simple until the mid-eighteenth century. Business organizations consisted mostly of family members who shared the responsibilities and worked for the common good. Their success was measured in the strictest terms of financial reward. However, with the advent of the Industrial Revolution, business moved from cottages to factories, employed large numbers of people and began to grow in both size and complexity. It was during this time that Adam Smith (1776) argued that by dividing labor into smaller, specialized tasks, efficiency would improve and production costs would decrease, and Robert Owen ([1815] 1977) wrote that managers should pay as much attention to the people of a company as to the machinery. Owen's work would later be identified as the beginning of the study of organizational dynamics and administration, which would examine how the efficiency of work contributions of individual or small, specialized groups related to the overall performance of the organization. This was the start of determining business performance in terms other than strictly financial, forever complicating the performance assessment process of business, and indirectly libraries.

While many administrators believe it to be a current development, the demand for organizations to harness greater amounts of performance, efficiency and value from the organizational structure and people has its roots in the advances in communications and technology during the late nineteenth and early twentieth centuries. Advances in technology and communication allowed businesses to access more distant markets that were previously closed to their goods. The size and complexity of organizations, their industrial plants and performance capabilities grew, and organizations serviced larger geographical areas of the world than the area surrounding the factory. Because of the broader global markets, business owners and managers found themselves in an increasingly competitive arena. Businesses which could produce large quantities of goods at the highest level of efficiency and thus at an affordable cost in a highly competitive market were deemed to be the most competitive and therefore the most successful, with success being measured solely on the scale of profitability for business owners and stockholders.

Obtaining greater amounts of efficiency and reducing cost in producing or providing goods and services became of paramount importance to business owners and stockholders during this expansion of global markets, as they believed that increased profitability was only possible through increased organizational efficiency and cost reduction. Much of the administrative and performance assessment research of the time was based on the prevailing perception of business administrators that increasingly higher levels of efficiency were possible, and more importantly necessary, to be competitive and maintain or increase profitability, which was still the key performance consideration. It was with the intent of generating the highest efficiency and reducing costs in the workplace that in 1885 Henry Metcalfe used his observational studies of soldiers in a military arsenal to advocate that the 'science of administration' would be beneficial to managers. Work organization research led to the field of 'scientific management': Louis Brandeis coined the phrase in 1910 when he stated before the Interstate Commerce Commission that through scientific management of resources and men, the nation's railroads could save over $1 million a day (Shafritz and Ott, 1997: 11).

While Brandeis may have coined the term 'scientific management', its philosophical father is considered to be Frederick Taylor (1911). Taylor conducted a series of scientific time and motion studies in the late 1890s and early 1900s on different groups of workers to determine the most efficient way to accomplish tasks, thus reducing costs. It is from Taylor's work, as well as that of other researchers, that many of today's performance assessment processes derive their scientific or analytical qualities. Scientific management researchers, such as Taylor, attempted to organize workers and resources into effective, scientific patterns of operation in order to improve production and reduce costs of an industrial or commercial plant. The organizing process focused on determining the most effective size and operation of an organization to maximize the quantity of work produced, not necessarily the quality of the work. Emphasis was placed on management's absolute control of the organization and its employees as the primary means to achieve increased productivity, efficiency and cost reduction. To determine the performance of organizations under this philosophy, managers measured the efficiency, degree of control and profitability of the organization. The high-quantity and high-control style of operations management and performance assessment continued through the early twentieth century up to the post-Second World War era.

The emphasis on scientific organizational control and optimization of the control and quantity of work slowly shifted to an emphasis on quality after the post-Second World War era. In the late 1950s and early 1960s advances in communications and technology were again providing the foundation for the expansion of the global economy. These advances allowed new competitors and products into older competitive markets where they had never been before. Because of increased competition, many business organizations seeking a competitive edge were forced to switch from a focus on providing and delivering large quantities of affordable but cheaply produced goods and services to a focus on providing and delivering high-quality goods and services.

The culture of business organizations was affected by this change to a competitive, quality-driven production philosophy. New organizational structures, values and practices that supported the competitive, quality production philosophy were encouraged, created and rewarded. New types of performance assessment methodologies and metrics were created to assist business owners and administrators in evaluating the production and service quality of their organizations, with the expectation of the organization becoming more competitive. It was during this period that quality-driven cost-accountability tools such as total quality control (TQC), total quality management (TQM), re-engineering and other similar tools became prevalent. Business organizations emphasized and prioritized the quality of work. The new quality-driven, cost-accountable performance measurement tools enhanced the administrator's ability to monitor the quality of production through tight control of resources, staff and processes. Costs were reduced and quality improved by using performance measurement information to identify problems and make corrective changes in organizational processes.

Competitive, quality-driven, cost-accountable performance assessment tools also enabled managers to address their stockholders' demands for accountability and quality performance by providing them with tangible and mutually understood performance information. Due to the increased service quality, profitability and/or access to accountability information, business customers and stockholders began appreciating the new competitive practices and assessments of quality management, and came to expect such competitive responses, accountability and quality assessment in the social and political aspects of their lives.

The competitive, quality-driven, cost-accountable production culture of businesses began to encroach on the overall societal culture in the mid-1990s, moving into all levels of government, community service groups and other non-profit service organizations. These cultural, non-profit service and governmental organizations began incorporating qualitative performance assessment methodologies and metrics into their traditional quantitative performance assessment systems to address stakeholder interests and requests for improved service value and impacts. The qualitative performance assessment systems were appealing to many cultural, governmental and non-profit service administrators and their stakeholders, as they faced growing numbers of incisive inquiries related to accountability and resource management.

Cultural, governmental and non-profit service administrators found it increasingly difficult to answer public concerns about the effective or efficient delivery of public services with traditional quantitative assessment systems and metrics alone, and were looking for new methods of reporting organizational performance. While traditional quantitative performance assessment could potentially demonstrate the cost-effectiveness of a non-profit organization, these measures alone could not provide many non-profit administrators with the necessary tools to address impact or compete for dwindling resources effectively. These administrators perceived that to respond to these impact inquires more effectively, the competitive, quality-driven, cost-accountable performance measures of the business world could be used to address whether the service provided was truly needed and what difference it made for its recipients. Non-profit organization administrators and stakeholders also perceived that just as businesses had adopted a quality-driven, cost-accountable culture and system, they could do so to improve their competitive abilities over other non-profit organizations in obtaining community and funding support.

It is against this background of business competition and assessment that libraries have formulated their performance assessment practices and metrics, especially as the library profession has predominately always adapted performance assessment processes and metrics from the business world to innovate its performance assessment capabilities.

Libraries have been attempting to demonstrate their performance and service value through performance assessment and metrics since the inception of public libraries in the eighteenth century. However, 'reliable and valid measurement in the social sciences is extremely difficult' (Wedgeworth, 1993: 547). While there have been many attempts and variations in the efforts to develop library performance measures, little progress has been made to date in establishing a systematic, universally accepted performance assessment system that effectively addresses all the inquiries of quality and cost accountability.

As stated earlier, performance assessment of organizational service and its quality is not a new development in libraries. The earliest assessment models in the late eighteenth century were based on distinct quantitative outputs and financial management of resources, just like the business assessment practices of the time. The traditional techniques of performance assessment developed during this early history of libraries included interviews, input/output analysis, cost analysis and activity analysis, which are still the most popular forms of performance assessment and service value metrics and reporting systems used in libraries today.

Lubans and Chapman (1975: 2) state that the innovation of performance assessment and service value in libraries began in 1876 with Cutter using cost-benefit analysis in a study of cataloging effectiveness. This continued with Shaw in the 1930s, who was one of the earliest practitioners and proponents of scientific management in the library profession. Shaw was an advocate of integration, using a 'total system approach' and 'reductions in workforce' to increase efficiency. Lubans and Chapman (ibid.) also describe how Rider used unit-cost study to maximize efficiency as early as 1934. In the late 1930s Rider was quoted as saying that 'if librarians did not use scientific management or cost benefit analysis (i.e. quantitative assessment information) to justify performance, non-librarians would come in and do it for us' (ibid.: 2) This statement was a hint of the competitive world that libraries face today and the situation in which many libraries find themselves.

Another innovation in library performance assessment was customer input in the assessment process, which was initiated in 1939 when Wilson became the first library professional to incorporate the use of customer surveys to determine organizational performance impact and accomplishment

7

(Hatry et al., 1979: 67). The inclusion of the customer in the library performance assessment process has generally seen better assessment results; however, overall Hatry et al. (ibid.) state: 'Most library systems lack information on: the level of citizen satisfaction with library operations, including the comfort of facilities, hours of operations, speed of service, and helpfulness of the staff; the availability of materials sought by the users; and the percentage of households using the system, with estimates of reasons for nonuse by those not using the system.' In 1986 the International Federation of Library Associations (IFLA) produced a consolidated collection of recommended minimal quantitative standards and measurements. Because these minimal standards were written to have the greatest application, IFLA cautioned readers that they were 'not likely to be universally relevant' to all libraries (International Federation of Library Associations, 1986: 61). The IFLA quantitative standards were soon in contradiction with the qualitative performance assessment developments being generally set by other library associations (i.e. the American Library Association, Chartered Institute of Library and Information Professionals, etc.). However, the use and predominance of quantitative performance assessment processes and metrics in libraries continue to this day.

In the 1950s and 1960s, as businesses began adopting quality-driven, cost-accountable performance measures, libraries also began to place more emphasis on transitioning their performance assessment to include qualitative measures. Qualitative performance assessment was not new to libraries at this time. In 1933 the American Library Association (ALA) became the first national library association to introduce qualitative standards of service. These qualitative standards had a broad scope to allow a wide range of acceptability by the profession. However, qualitative service standards alone were seen as having limited benefit to libraries as a benchmark against which to measure quantitative performance and service value.

Initially, according to Ammons (2000: 211), these qualitative standards of service prescribed 'appropriate levels of financial support and staff credentials'. The standards contained phrasing that provided little specific information to facilitate measuring performance by professionals or the community at large. Ammons (ibid.: 212) continues by stating that the qualitative standards 'offered little leverage for prying resources from the city [county] treasury. In short, they [standards] failed to arm library administrators with a persuasive means of demonstrating to budget makers local shortcomings in facilities, services, and funding.'

The change in emphasis to qualitative performance assessment in libraries has caused concern among those who still feel the need to have quantitative performance standards. Kaplan (2001) states that library administrators and stakeholders are becoming increasingly aware that financial performance measures alone are not sufficient to evaluate organizational performance. Stakeholders and communities are increasingly pressuring libraries to respond strategically more effectively to local needs and changes. Historically, the profession has more frequently adopted new performance assessment processes and metrics from outside the library profession (i.e. the business world), with negligible innovation in developing performance assessment processes or metrics within the library profession. The benefits derived by libraries using these adapted performance assessment processes and metrics have not been fully examined to date.

Examples of the most noted assessment processes and metrics adopted from outside the library profession include benchmarking, outcomes-based evaluation, Six Sigma, TQM or other strongly quantitative measurements such as the balanced scorecard (BSC), and a variety of customer

Table 1.1 Common performance assessment processes

Service organizational type	Commonly used performance assessments (efficiency/ effectiveness)	Commonly used performance assessments (valuation)
Service-driven (for-profit business)	ISO Standards Malcolm Baldridge (for-profit model) TQM methodologies (i.e. TQM, TQP, TCM) Benchmarking Kaizen Six Sigma Balanced scorecard Competitive intelligence Efficiency measures from operations management (i.e. capacity, utilization)	Total cost of ownership (TCO) Return on investment (ROI) Return on assets (ROA) Cost avoidance Intellectual capital Human capital Structural capital Customer capital Process capital Financial capital Community capital
Service-driven (non-profit/ library)	Malcolm Baldridge (educational model) Output/efficiency measures TQM methodologies (i.e. TQM, TQP, TCM) Goals/objectives Performance-based budgeting ServQual/LibQual Benchmarking Balanced scorecard	Expert valuation** Cost avoidance* ROI* Outcomes-based evaluation**
Technology service-driven (for-profit business)	Outputs Server counts Transactional log analysis Log-ins Capacity Number of users Demographics of users Number of pages hit Balanced scorecard Organizational alignment Knowledge management Competitive intelligence Efficiency measures from operations management (i.e. capacity, utilization)	Intellectual capital Human capital Structural capital Customer capital Process capital Financial capital Community capital TCO ROI/ROA Cost avoidance

* Not routinely performed.
** Not universally employed at this date.

satisfaction measurement systems like LibQual. Table 1.1 gives a comparison of the more common types of performance and value assessments used in for-profit, non-profit/library and technology service organizations.

Current status and issues in performance assessment

The current issues in developing and using performance assessment (i.e. for service quality, customer service, resource accountability, use of technology, etc.) generate great discussion in the literature of the library profession, as many libraries are feeling the pressure from their stakeholders continually to redefine and improve their abilities to report performance information.

The use of quantitative standards of service alone has proven to be of controversial and limited benefit to libraries since their inception in the 1930s, with some of the negative aspects including their being created without consideration of the different service needs of individual communities; not supporting larger or top-echelon libraries in their efforts to demonstrate performance (the larger and top-echelon libraries are often penalized when their performance results exceed the standards, providing local officials with 'justification' to divert library funding to other agencies); and not systematically approaching performance assessment from the perspective of library customers or potential customers.

Qualitative performance assessment processes and metrics have been equally of generally limited benefit to libraries. The information derived from these qualitative processes addresses the long-term 'big picture' assessment of quality and value of a library's services and competitive responses. However, they do not provide the quantitative information needed by administrators and stakeholders about daily operations and efficiency to address competitive response needs. In essence, library administrators need an effective mixture of both quantitative and qualitative processes and metrics to address all their performance assessment information needs, as having timely and competitive quality and operational assessment information is essential for library administrators in making effective strategic decisions and allocating resources.

In further examining the current status of performance assessment in libraries, another major issue affecting the use and innovation of assessment processes and metrics is the lack of consensus among members of the profession as to the purpose of performance assessment and the metrics that should be used. For example, Lancaster (1977) states that performance measurement consists of micro-evaluation, which is how a system operates and why, and macro-evaluation, which is how well a system operates. Van House et al. (1987) suggest that the primary utility of performance measures is for internal staff diagnosis and use. They state that 'performance measurement serves several purposes in libraries: assessing current levels of performance; diagnosing possible problem areas; comparing current and desired levels of performance; and monitoring progress' (ibid.: 2), with the major benefit of performance assessment being 'that it provides information for planning and decision-making' (ibid.: 3). As library administrators and stakeholders are facing increased competition for services and resources, performance assessment is being transitioned into a tool to support the library's strategic and competitive responses. Library administrators are looking to introduce more complex quantitative performance assessment processes and metrics that blend qualitative aspects of organizational performance and value with the more traditional quantitative library performance and efficiency in order to respond to accountability concerns from stakeholders.

In addition to the lack of consensus on the purpose of performance assessment, there is a lack of consensus in the measures to be used in the assessment process. For example, according to Van House et al. (ibid.) there are three types of performance measures used by libraries: inputs, outputs and productivity. Input measures are described as the resources (human, financial and material) and costs of producing and delivering library services and products. Output measures fall within three categories: quantity, quality and timeliness. Output measures are geared to provide data on the overall quantities of service and products provided, the financial cost of the service and products and the speed of the service. Kraft and Boyce (1991) determined four types of library performance measures that library administrators should employ to address stakeholder inquiries:

- the amounts of resources libraries have at their disposal;
- the efficiency in using these resources to generate services;
- the effectiveness in how alternatives are used to meet goals;
- the benefit to society and the library environment.

Risher and Fay (1995) suggest that performance assessment metrics should measure anything that is important to at least one group of library stakeholders, and should illustrate the timeliness and variation of service the organization is capable of accomplishing and customer satisfaction. Finally, Hernon and Altman (1998: 27) state that performance measures 'characterize the extent, effectiveness, and efficiency of library programs and services'. So, as one can see, there is a wide perception of what performance assessment metrics are and how they should be used by libraries. When the issue of these multiple perceptions is combined with the fact that many library administrators do not understand performance assessment processes nor value the results, this leaves little enthusiasm and commitment to allocate dwindling staff and resources to innovate performance assessment processes and metrics. Lacking consensus in purposes and metrics also leaves those with doubts or little knowledge of the process with no direction, and information needs with no platform of safety to step out on to explore. Lacking consensus also provides an excuse for those library administrators who do not value the process and its results not to use or pursue new performance assessment processes and metrics. Seeing no progress or options in sight, many library administrators will continue to use the tested, traditional assessment processes and metrics, even when they do not provide the best information for making strategic decisions or allocating resources, because they are safe and familiar to library staff and stakeholders.

Another current issue in the use of performance assessment in libraries is the increasing complexity and scope of the library's services and delivery systems. Technology allows library services to be enjoyed in the library, in the community and throughout the world wherever the customer needs to access the services. Libraries are providing more intangible services and using more intangible resources than ever before, and these are difficult to assess or value. The library's missions and strategic requirements by stakeholders are broadening the scope of services provided and, in conjunction with technology, are increasing the numbers and locations of people interacting with or receiving services from the library. As the scope of what is required from the library and how it is delivered continues to increase, assessing the library's services is becoming more complicated and requires more sophisticated resources, tools and time to undertake effectively. With libraries facing dwindling resources to provide and assess services, it is understandable that many library administrators do not want to commit resources to using or innovating performance assessment when they are needed in daily operations.

When one overlays the quantitative/qualitative performance assessment discussion and the need for increased competitive responses from libraries on top of the results of a lack of consensus on the purpose of performance assessment and the types of metrics to use, plus dwindling staff and financial resources to allocate to potentially non-beneficial activities (i.e. performance assessment), the end result for the profession is the 'perfect storm' (i.e. where all of the conditions are perfect for something to go very wrong) of negative circumstances in which to develop, innovate and implement performance assessment processes and metrics. In this perfect storm environment, one can understand why some libraries have not seen clearly enough any benefit in performance assessment processes and innovations or in developing their own processes and metrics. And this 'perfect storm' could not be occurring at a worse time for libraries; just as library administrators and stakeholders are being required to produce more performance assessment information to address an increasingly competitive service environment and compete for dwindling resources, the use of performance assessment in libraries seems without innovation and direction.

Challenges to using library performance assessment information to make strategic decisions

The literature on library performance assessment suggests that there are many challenges affecting the profession's abilities to utilize this assessment effectively. The most noted challenge is the indifference that many library administrators have towards conducting performance assessment and the derived value of the process. The Institute for Museum and Library Services (IMLS, 2000: 2) states that 'Ambivalence toward evaluation is widely recognized and shared by many professional leaders.' White (2002) found that many library administrators not only viewed the performance assessment process and its results with indifference, but actually disliked, under-resourced and underutilized performance assessment and its resulting information, as it was viewed as a non-beneficial process that took time away from serving customers. If the leader of performance assessment (i.e. the library administrator) does not value and promote the process or allocate the necessary resources to perform it effectively, the library staff and stakeholders will not value the process and its results either. Thus the library administration and stakeholders do not have the essential information to make strategic decisions, compete for and allocate resources, and effectively address the community's needs.

An associated category of challenge to using performance assessment and its resulting information to make strategic decisions is the lack of administrators' understanding of how to use assessment effectively in their libraries. Libraries do not usually have the resources (or do not have them allocated for performance assessment) to support an administrative or staff team or individuals who are solely dedicated to performance assessment and specially trained to conduct this assessment and interpret or act on the results. Additionally many library practitioners do not have an understanding of organizational systems, thus sometimes in the effort to improve one performance measure, they adversely affect another measure. An example of this challenge is a library which decides to increase the technology training of customers and expand or strengthen access to the library's communications infrastructure to provide faster or greater access to its electronic information resources for customers outside the library. In response, more customers learn how to and do utilize the electronic information sources from outside the traditional library building and do not come into the library, thus decreasing the library's circulation and customer activity data. As resources are awarded based on the library's activity data, a decrease in activity could result in a negative financial resource allocation for the positively received effort. Having a proper understanding of the library as a system and of the use of performance assessment is essential to be able to describe system performance effectively.

Another challenge in libraries using performance assessment to make strategic decisions is the perception that the assessment processes and metrics are not customer-driven and are frequently misused as a tool of accountability instead of a true assessment tool. This perception of not being customer-focused owes its existence in part to the common and current practices of libraries to use forms of performance assessment processes and metrics that are almost entirely internally focused. So while many libraries include customers in surveys of service or need, and provide final drafts of the results of performance assessment in a reporting process (most of the time), customers and key stakeholders as a whole are not included in the overall performance assessment processes (i.e. not involved in assessment design, data collection and design, interpretation/analysis and reporting). Thus they feel excluded from the process, which is the evidence portion of the service relationship between the library and its customers and stakeholders. This relational disconnect promotes uncertainty, miscommunication and misunderstanding between the library and its customers and stakeholders; the result of which is an ever-increasing effort by the library to provide evidence of value and impact to its customer and stakeholder audience.

As libraries are being required to provide greater amounts of performance assessment information to customers and stakeholders, library staff and administrators are being required to commit more effort into learning and using multiple performance assessment processes. This becomes a challenge to using performance assessment information to make strategic decisions. Lawes (1993: 142) states that 'many libraries have been measuring so many [different] output measures for so long in so many different ways that staff frequently suffer from a "mental paralysis"'. Due to long-term exposure to the multiple measurement process, poor understanding of procedures and interpretation and an inability to see value in learning and using new performance assessment processes, administrators and staff lose interest, focus and energy; thus errors are introduced into the data collection, or the results are not implemented as effectively as they should be due to the resulting apathy and confusion.

The apathy and confusion resulting from the 'mental paralysis' is described by Lakos (1999) as a dichotomy of performance assessment perceptions and values: the value of providing service versus the value of providing the information needed to address library competition, strategic decision-making and accountability. Many library practitioners and administrators view the delivery of service as being of greater value than any assessment effort, and tend to treat the performance assessment either like a regularly scheduled yearly event (i.e. an event or something on my to-do list) or overemphasize the process of performance assessment, overwhelming all those who might benefit from the intended results.

Libraries' organizational structures can also create challenges to the ability to use performance assessment information to make strategic decisions. Halachmi and Bouckaert (1996) state that the unsuccessful deployment of performance assessment is inherent in the nature of the organizational structure and culture of libraries. They identified four primary groups of organizational structure factors that prevent libraries from using performance assessment successfully.

- Institutional cultural factors, such as resistance to change, procedural and policy dependency and impediments, professional standards and philosophies, rigid organizational structures and a lack of a culture of assessment.

- Pragmatic factors, such as employees' ability to improve, their ability to learn and use the measures correctly, and overcoming organizational cultural artifacts from other previous performance assessment processes.

- Technical factors, such as maintaining access to ever-changing technologies, skills to use technology in performance assessment, innovation of measures and knowing the effective techniques of measurement.

- Cost factors, such as the costs of measuring performance and lost service time or productivity by staff.

Another aspect of organizational structure challenge for libraries is their funding system. 'The third-party payer system ... reinforces the service culture [for library administrators]. Government funding and contracts tend to reward previously proven methods, not innovations. Funders want to back successful programs and often won't signal dissatisfaction as long as the money is "well spent" and accounted for' (Letts et al., 1999: 34). The last aspect of the organizational structure challenge, as stated by Kanter and Summers (1987), is the argument that as the economy, society and people evolve, for-profit and non-profit organizations will evolve towards each other. Changes over the past five years have created a situation where 'the lines dividing for-profit and not-for-profit organizations with respect to performance measurement are blurring' (ibid.: 380). For-profit bodies are becoming more socially conscious, creating social missions and values for their organizations, while non-profit organizations are setting more stringent quantitative measures and using more strategic measurement of their performance and services. This blurring of the lines between for-profit and not-for-profit organizations is especially a reality facing libraries, for reasons stated earlier in this chapter. A current example is frequently found in England; the blurred (i.e. for-profit and non-profit) organizational structure is becoming common in many governmental and public service agencies. Libraries were one of the first governmental/social agencies to participate in the concept of the blurred structure. One library model, called 'best value', was implemented in early 1999. Libraries were asked not only to account for service quality but also to 'define the values for money and quality of service delivery' (Liddle, 1999: 206). 'The four "Cs" measured the program: this included Challenge, is the service needed at all?; Compare, involving analysis, comparison, and benchmarking; Consult, which requires authorities to seek dialogue with the public it serves; and Compete, which looks for partnerships and private sector involvement' (ibid.).

The final challenge for libraries using performance assessment information to make strategic decisions is the implied amount of precision in performance measures. This implied precision may affect a library administrator's decision-making by lending credibility to performance assessment results or outcomes that may not be merited due to ineffective/incorrect efforts or process errors, thus making ineffective or detrimental strategic decisions or resource allocations that may adversely affect the library's strategic and competitive success. This lack of precision was most notably described by the team of DeProspo et al., who worked on a library output measures project in 1973. After experiencing many questions and problems from practitioners while completing their project, the team concluded that 'the profession had no widely accepted [or precise] definitions of library goodness or how to measure it effectively. Until these [definitions] are established, all such measurement/comparison efforts are groping in the dark' (Lynch, 1990: 5).

The lack of precision in the information resulting from performance assessment is sometimes created by the timing of assessment processes in libraries. Many library performance assessments are scheduled yearly or as needed, and are not ongoing processes or structured to function continuously for specific ongoing critical performance assessment information needs of library administrators. Additionally, most assessment processes are reactive in nature, with very few being predictive. The result of this timing scenario is that library administrators react from a more defensive posture in conducting and using performance assessment, and this limits the effectiveness and benefits of the assessment process and its resulting information.

Alignment of performance assessment processes and metrics to library assessment information needs can affect the precision of the process and its resulting information. If the processes and metrics are not strategically aligned to match results to the library decision-maker's strategic needs, regardless of how effectively obtained and reported, the information will not precisely meet the library administrator's needs to allow strategic decisions to be made.

Another source of imprecision in performance measurement comes from within the library profession. Many library practitioners and administrators have failed to keep up with the advancements in performance assessment methodologies, technologies and terminologies related to the library profession or to industries outside of the profession, e.g. business, computer science, information technology and for-profit service-driven businesses. This is evidenced in White's (2002) study of library administrators, in which many reported using older performance assessment methods and metrics even when they did not align with the changing requirements of reporting performance assessment to stakeholders, dwindling resources and the changing service environment (i.e. the geographic area of service the library is charged/wants to serve).

Against the backdrop of these challenges to using performance assessment information to make strategic decisions, the library's organizational structure will continue to blur; its purpose and service delivery will continue to be dynamic or expand in scope; competition for service, customers and resources will increase; and its stakeholders will become more diverse in need and location. Performance assessment as it is currently practiced in libraries will become more difficult to use effectively and benefit from in strategic decision-making.

Future needs

Given the current competitive service environments and challenges to using existing performance assessment processes in libraries for use in strategic decision-making, the future of libraries will depend greatly on generating more effective strategic responses. Updating the existing assessment processes and metrics used in libraries to obtain more competitive service environment information is essential to improving the process of generating strategic responses. To begin the innovation process, there are three major focal points for the profession to address: incorporating performance assessment into strategic and operational planning and resource allocation; increasing practitioner and administrator understanding of performance assessment; and aligning the new/existing performance assessment processes and metrics to fit better in the strategic service environment in which most libraries operate.

Including performance assessment processes in long-range, strategic and tactical/operational planning is critical to providing strong organizational support for the assessment process and its results. Libraries frequently do not include performance assessment in their structured or strategic planning processes and seldom dedicate resources exclusively to supporting the assessment processes (i.e. design, data collection and data analysis) in budgets. By including performance assessment and its resources into the larger strategic planning of the library, administrators would be sending a message that effective performance assessment is essential to the library and its future. If something is essential enough for library administrators to plan and allocate resources to it, then it is important enough for staff to support and conduct as effectively as possible. Furthermore, providing increased and structured support for the performance assessment process would allow the library to identify and incorporate the most effective outside assessment theory, practice and metrics or the internal innovation of existing metrics and processes. This integrated planning and structured resource support of performance assessment by library administrators further builds confidence in the value of results of the assessment processes for library staff, customers and stakeholders, which aids library administrators' efforts and credibility in reporting performance to library stakeholders.

As part of the strategic planning and resource allocation support, investment in the library administration and staff to increase the understanding, value and use of performance assessment processes and metrics is critical. Whether all the performance assessment process is conducted internally by library staff and administrators or externally by outside contractors/consultants and overseen by library personnel, increasing the understanding of the assessment's use and value by library staff and administrators seems an integral component to improving the effectiveness and use of performance assessment information in making strategic decisions and resource allocations.

The last focal point of aligning existing and new performance assessment processes and metrics to the competitive service environment of libraries is critical for library administrators and stakeholders. One of the first alignments between the assessment processes and the service environment is for the library to take advantage of one of the strengths of the abundant technology (i.e. counting) available in/to most libraries. Using technology to automate the performance assessment processes would increase the use, collecting, analysis and reporting of the resulting information. In addition to reducing resource and staff time commitments, automated performance assessment processes and metrics would be potentially more proactive, consistently collected and analyzed, readily available for library use and capable of running continuously while reducing bias input from library personnel in the process. Further, having a more technology-automated assessment process is less intrusive for the customer in assessing daily customer transactions, yet would expand access to the performance assessment processes by customers and stakeholders who are increasingly using the library via electronic means.

An alignment between library performance assessment processes and stakeholder accountability information needs is also required in the future in order for the library to provide performance assessment information more effectively to its customers and stakeholders. Research has shown that libraries do not always involve strategic stakeholders in the assessment processes (sometimes not even as a reporting audience); this has especially been noted in the critical performance assessment process area of determining the specifics of the amounts and types of information needed to respond effectively to inquiries about accountability from customers and stakeholders.

For example, a library can provide a key stakeholder with abundant and effective amounts of qualitative data about its impact on community illiteracy levels, with customer testimonials and outcomes evidence to support the library's value and efforts. However, if the key stakeholder (especially if it is a funding source) processes performance assessment data strictly in the quantitative terms of cost-benefit analysis or return on investment, the library's performance assessment information is not understood or valued, cannot be integrated into the funding source's performance assessment system and will not be a competitive or effective response to inquiries about accountability or value in the eyes of the key stakeholder. It is critical that at the onset of each performance assessment, the library ensures that the process it plans to use produces the types and amounts of the effectiveness, accountability and value information needed and understood by customers and stakeholders. Otherwise, the resources used to conduct performance assessment and the value generated by the assessment process are wasted.

Another performance assessment alignment needed is to focus more of the assessment process and information sources on external aspects of the service environment and value/impact creation. Having an in-depth knowledge of the library's operations and internal performance is still critical, but knowing about the library alone is not enough; the library needs to know more about the community it serves or is underserving.

Traditionally, library performance assessment has been internally focused and more oriented to reporting efficiency/effectiveness rather than value/impact created. The result of this internal/efficiency focus has been limited success in generating effective strategic responses and demonstrating value for libraries. Learning more about the service environment in which the library and its customers (and potential customers) interact and how competitors operate and provide value to the library's customers or impact the library's service environment is critical strategic information that is necessary to understanding that environment. In the increasingly competitive service market in which libraries are operating, aligning the library's performance assessment processes and metrics to identify and measure the library's value/impact creation will be potentially more powerful and essential for library administrators, especially in the provision of strategic information for generating strategic responses.

Generating effective strategic responses potentially creates greater value and impact in the library's service environment. However, to know whether the library's strategic responses are generating value or impact, the question has to be asked, 'What are your library's service environment impacts?' The answers are essential in order for the library to address requests for evidence of impact or value from the library. Why? Because the library's customers, stakeholders and competitors already know the library's value and impact; maybe not in exact terms, but they all have some sense of what the value and impact of the library and its services are to them, and they expect the library to know this and be able to respond by showing service responsiveness to needs and accountability of the resources invested in it by the community it serves.

Identifying service environment impacts

As has been reviewed, service environment value and impact are becoming more frequent key stakeholder performance inquiries for libraries and their administrators to address in generating strategic responses and decision-making. Traditional library performance assessment does not effectively provide all of the information from the service environment needed by library administrators to generate strategic responses and make effective strategic decisions. In order to change this, the competitive library will have to innovate its performance assessment processes to obtain the performance and competitive information required by library administrators. The library of the future will need to be able effectively to identify and generate strategic responses in its service environment that create positive value and impacts if it expects to be a competitive force in its service environment. In identifying and determining the value/impact of the library, it will also need to know more about all of the service environment contributors and their values/impact, as this will further strengthen the library's understanding of its own impact and value and allow for the development of more effective strategic decisions and responses. But how can the library do this?

The first part of the answer to that question is to understand better how to align performance assessment effectively, which is covered in Chapter 2. However, even with a more aligned and effective performance assessment process, libraries need to know more about their competitive library service environment. The second part of the answer is learning more about the library and its competitors, which begins with an overview of library service competition in Chapter 3. Chapters 4–7 provide guidance on the types of information the library must 'know' and how the library can begin to use the information gathered from competitive and performance assessment processes to generate strategic information and responses to be more competitive in its service environments.

2

Aligning the performance assessment process

As stated previously, a major way to improve the current performance assessment process to allow the library to compete more effectively in its service environment is to increase the alignment of the assessment process. To create an effective performance assessment process for a library and its service environment, it is important to align the components of the assessment process with the library and the components of the service environment to give the maximum value and effectiveness in the performance assessment effort. Figure 2.1 depicts the performance assessment process components in the library's service environment.

The assessment alignment model illustrates how all the six assessment components are interrelated: the library, customers/stakeholders, capacity/utilization, assessment, technology and participation. Each component operates simultaneously as a separate component and in conjunction with the other components while interacting directly with the library's service environment.

The library, at the center of the assessment alignment model, provides the necessary organizational and resource support for the assessment process and communicates the external value and impact to customers/stakeholders. The library is the primary communication link to the customers, stakeholders, other alignment components and the external service

Figure 2.1 Components of aligning library performance assessment

Library's competitive service environment

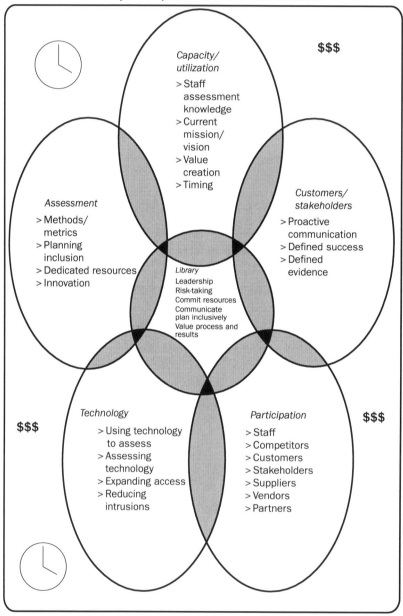

environment. Being in such a pivotal position, it is essential for the library's administrators to develop and contribute to effective performance assessment alignment in several ways.

- Communicating with the components of the library's service environment and the customers and stakeholders regarding their performance assessment information needs and the resulting information.

- Communicating performance assessment needs/priorities/ results to the library's internal customers (i.e. staff, volunteers, collaborators/partners, vendors, suppliers, etc.).

- Using evidence-based decision-making which utilizes the results and knowledge obtained from the library's performance assessment processes in all tactical and strategic planning, goal-setting and tactical/operational decisions.

- Creating trust in the integrity of the library's performance assessment practices and the veracity of the resulting information for internal and external customers and all stakeholders.

- Demonstrating organizational commitment to the need and importance of the library performance assessment through dedicated resources, staff and training provided to support the processes.

- Supporting performance assessment practice/metrics innovation within the library and identifying and adopting innovative practices/metrics from outside of the library that indicate they would complement or benefit the library's processes.

The most critical component of the performance assessment alignment model is the customers/stakeholders. Customers and stakeholders determine organizational direction and provide the needs that the library must fill in order to be determined efficient/effective/of value to the service environment. Customers and stakeholders help the library administration to determine the appropriate performance assessment processes and evidentiary metrics, which drive the other assessment alignment components. These determinations in turn form the basis of the library's strategic and operational processes, and decide how its success will be defined and measured, and how the library will be perceived (in both strategic and tactical terms) by customers, stakeholders and the library's service environment in terms of resource allocations and strategic success. The library can develop effective assessment process alignment with customers and stakeholders in a variety of ways.

- Proactively engaging customers and stakeholders (internally and externally) in open communication to ascertain their definition(s) of success and the specific type(s) of data/evidence/knowledge needed by key customers and stakeholders.

- Making the performance assessment process transparent for customers and stakeholders in terms of understanding the metrics, practices, reporting and results.

- Providing all customers and stakeholders with the opportunity to participate in the assessment process (identifying required evidence, process and metrics selection, and data collection, analysis and reporting).

Another component of the alignment model is the capacity/utilization of the library to perform assessment processes. The library must have the capacity (whether through its own resources or outside resources) to understand the concepts of performance assessment and its use in library systems and operations, and to develop, innovate or identify non-library performance assessment resources that could provide benefit to the library's assessment processes. The library must also have the ability to utilize the necessary performance assessment processes, metrics and tools, and to use the resulting data/information/knowledge in strategic and tactical decision-making, planning and resource allocation. The library can develop effective performance assessment process alignment using its capacity and utilization in three ways.

- Continuously updating the performance assessment skills/understanding of the library staff, leadership, customers and stakeholders.

- Conducting regular performance assessment skill/resource inventories to determine needed skills/resources to be either developed internally or obtained from outside providers.

- Acquiring and allocating the resources (both within and outside the library) necessary to conduct performance assessment effectively within the library and in the library's service environment.

As stated earlier, performance assessment itself is one of the alignment components needed in the library service environment. This component is the central foundation from which the library's performance assessment processes originate, operate and produce the needed information and knowledge to make effective strategic decisions. The library's performance assessment processes can be aligned most effectively with the information needs of library administrators, customers and stakeholders by the following means.

- Designing performance assessment processes that most effectively provide the strategic and tactical information required by library administrators, customers and stakeholders.

- Developing multiple options for obtaining and validating required assessment information in regular or continuous processes.

- Using processes and metrics that customers and stakeholders approve of and can easily understand and appreciate.

- Using processes and metrics understood and capable of being administered by staff or outside assessment providers.

- Using processes and metrics that support the library's available resources to conduct performance assessment.

- Continuously innovating resources, processes and metrics.

- Focusing equally on the process of how performance assessment is conducted and the effectiveness of the results and their usage.

- Evaluating the performance assessment processes and employed metrics of the library regularly, including the evaluation results in future performance assessment design and implementation, to determine if the processes provide needed data/results for strategic/tactical decision-making, planning and resource allocations; provide the needed information and results to address customers' and stakeholders' value and impact information requirements; produce more answers than questions; effectively use the resources available to the process; deliver the library strategic/tactical successes in the service environment; and effectively report all the library's organizational performance and value created (including intangible assets and performance if appropriate for addressing customer and stakeholder concerns).

The technology component of the alignment model is the most dynamic component in the library performance assessment process due to three factors: the degree of integration that technology has with all other aspects of the delivery of library and information services makes it difficult to assess directly (especially in remote-access library services); the speed and frequent change of technology's applications and abilities require frequent changes in performance assessment processes and metrics; and there is a need to identify the most effective practices and methods of using technology in conducting the library's performance assessment. The library can develop effective process alignment using its technology in several ways.

- Using effective and proven technologies in combination with a proper understanding of how customers interact with and access the library's services.

- Applying technology in the performance assessment process in ways that enhance the value of the process (i.e. automate assessment processes that are effective/efficient: automating an ineffective assessment practice/method will only get bad results faster).

- Assessing the library's technology using the latest innovations from inside and outside the library service environment.

- Assessing those technologies that measure usage as well as added value/impact for library customers outside the library facility.

The participation component of the performance assessment alignment model is usually the most misaligned component. Organizational administrators and stakeholders frequently either involve outside considerations (politics, personalities, etc.) or ignore the component altogether. Involving the right person or group in the performance assessment can be one of the most pivotal decisions in the process. Not allowing participation or allowing only limited participation in the full assessment process to all interested parties can lead to partial/biased results and a lack of veracity and support in the process. Involving disinterested, uninformed or malevolent persons or groups in the performance assessment can overly complicate or invalidate the process results for the library, wasting resources and reducing stakeholder capital while creating an ineffective performance assessment process. Conversely, involving interested, informed or well-intentioned persons or groups in the performance assessment can reduce complications and validate the process results for the library, make effective use of limited assessment resources and increase stakeholder capital while creating an effective assessment process and library operation. The library can develop effective process alignment participation in several ways.

- Actively encouraging stakeholder input into the performance assessment process design and in defining what success is for the library before implementing the process.

- Engaging customers and stakeholders in all locations of the library's service environment (those served solely inside the library, those served solely by remote access to services and those served in both ways), using technology to close the distance and participation gaps.

- Including the most qualified internal or external stakeholders/customers within the performance assessment process (design, implementation, analysis and reporting/ dissemination).

- Including library staff (all levels), volunteers, collaborators, suppliers, vendors, etc. in the process where the relationship between the group and the library's performance assessment is most direct and beneficial for both parties.

- Identifying those assessment processes and metrics that add the most value to the key customers and stakeholders in those activities.

- Disseminating the value, participation and results of the performance assessment to all aspects of the service environment and internal/external stakeholders, including all interested/affected parties in the dissemination.

- Celebrating the participation and successes of performance assessment in the library, including all internal/external customers and stakeholders; everyone loves to be a part of a success.

By increasing the alignment of the library's performance assessment process to its competitive service environment using the model's components, the library can obtain more effective information to develop strategic responses. The alignment of the performance assessment process also allows the library to integrate the library and its services to the service environment, thus injecting increased value and impact into the service environment. Both of these benefits allow the library to become a stronger competitive force in its service environment. But, exactly how competitive is the library's service environment? An overview is provided in Chapter 3.

3

A concise overview of current library service competition

The library service environment has become much more competitive over the past 30 years, with a major form of competition coming from the advances of technology and the information economy. But technology is not the only or even the most visible form of competition for library services. Competition in the library service environment comes in all shapes and sizes, and can even be invisible to the library and its customers.

Current status and issues

The competition in the library service environment is composed of three primary forces: competition for providing services, competition for customers and competition for operational resources. Competition for providing library services (or services frequently provided by libraries) comes from for-profit, non-profit and other governmental bodies. The major for-profit competitors include:

- electronic information service providers (i.e. database and article content vendors, information search engines like Google and Yahoo!, entertainment resources like downloadable audiovisual resources, internet/communications service providers and social-presence websites like YouTube or Facebook);

- companies directly competing for the provision of library services in their own service environment (companies like Library Systems and Services, which provides stakeholders with options for the staffing, operations and technology of libraries or for the partial or total outsourcing all of library services);

- vendors which retail or otherwise provide library-style resources and services (i.e. bookstores, video/music stores, photocopying, faxing, internet cafes, newspaper stands, publishers and online booksellers like Amazon.com).

These for-profit competitors are very visible and form a defined competitive force in the library services environment. Library customers and potential customers know and value these competitors as they have high-recognition brand names and regular introductions of innovative services or products, are easy to do business with and provide the customer with nearly unlimited choices in meeting their library/information service needs.

The major non-profit competitors in the library service environment include:

- social service information providers (i.e. non-profit organizations that promote information resources, literacy resources and skills, technology access and training);

- other libraries in the service environment (customers can and frequently do have access to the resources and services of multiple libraries) or outside the service environment (i.e. libraries that are intended to serve specialized or large audiences, like national libraries/archives, and regional/ cooperative libraries offering services that overlap a smaller library's service environment);

- educational or well-being activities organizations (i.e. public or private organizations that provide activities or programs for community residents such as childcare centers, after-school programs, summer camps, community centers, social clubs, recreational centers like the YMCA, private schools, literacy centers, etc.) offering learning and development activities that many library customers can access instead of or in combination with the library's services.

The non-profit competitors can be nearly invisible to the library and the customer, and form a dynamic and not always predictable competitive force in the service environment. Library customers and potential customers know and value these competitors primarily in need-driven or opportunity situations, tending to use the non-profit organizations for library and information resources and services as their needs and opportunities dictate. This can make these bodies and the library customer's use of them hard for the library to identify and directly respond to strategically. These competitors are usually highly accessible and convenient for library customers to access, and provide supplemental service opportunities focusing on small or large community needs that the library may not be able to meet effectively in its resources and services.

The major governmental competitors in the library service environment include:

- publicly funded schools and literacy/educational organizations and programs providing activities, resources and programs that are similar to library services;
- governmental organizations that create and deliver their own information resources and services;
- information and referral centers established by government to assist and educate the community about governmental information, resources and services.

Governmental competitors in the library service environment are usually well-defined organizations with limited missions. These competitors can be nearly invisible to the library and its customers, and form a stable but limited competitive force in the library services environment. Library customers and potential customers have limited knowledge of these governmental competitors, primarily as they face limited resource support and narrow audiences or missions in providing information referral or other services similar to library services. These factors can make these organizations and the library customer's use of them hard for the library to identify and directly respond to strategically. The governmental competitors usually have limited access and convenience for library customers, with services that focus on a very narrow scope and appeal to a limited audience.

As stated earlier, competition for providing library services (or services frequently provided by libraries) comes from for-profit, non-profit and other governmental competitors. While each type of for-profit competitor brings similar competitive strategic considerations for the library (i.e. provides services and resources similar to library services and resources), the greater competitive challenge for many libraries is in determining how to respond strategically to these competitors: many are invisible to the library and its customers, do not have to be directly located within the library's service environment to have a competitive impact and serve as collaborators (or potential collaborators) with libraries to provide services and value to the library's customers and the community it serves. Creating library competitive responses that adversely affect or do not consider the impacts on library collaborators (or future collaborators) may in turn actually make the competition more difficult to respond to for libraries and their stakeholders.

Competition for customers in the library service environment has visible and invisible components. Library customers and potential customers have more library and information service choices (not only from libraries but from those competitors mentioned previously) than ever before, and the choices continue to grow daily. In addition to the ability to choose from multiple library and information service providers, actual and potential library customers have multiple and flexible choices of when to access these services, from where to access them, the technologies used in access, the costs of access, being on the innovative edge of available services and the control they can exert over the access to services.

The biggest strategic challenge for library administrators posed by this form of competitive force is the awareness of these choice options among library customers and key stakeholders. Customers and stakeholders know they have the ability increasingly to demand additional services (and value) from the library (as from other information service providers), as they have many service options open to them providing access choices, innovative services and increased service value. Yet the customer is not always aware or does not always understand why the library does not have the totality of resources and strategic capacity to provide the choices, innovation and access to services they are demanding. Library administrators frequently get caught in this customer and stakeholder awareness gap, which leads to the library being unable to obtain or provide the resources necessary to meet the increased service demand or provide evidence of service impact and value to demonstrate its efforts in responding to service demands.

In terms of what the library's customers are aware of, here is a reality check for libraries and library administrators to think about.

- The library is not the *only* provider of library and information services in the service environment.

- The library may not even be the *best* provider of library and information services in the service environment.

- The library may not be the *first* provider I think of when obtaining library and information services.

- Someone can take *me* (the customer) away from the library if *you* let them. And they are trying!

These reality checks have been shared with many library administrators over time, and many of them had not viewed the service environment from the customer's perspective before encountering these checks. It is critical that more library administrators take customer (and potential customer) awareness into consideration when making strategic decisions and allocating resources to provide effective library services, in order to close the customer awareness gap and increase the library's competitive position in its service environment.

The visible components of competitors for library customers include:

- the existing for-profit, non-profit and other governmental competitors previously discussed;

- organizations or activities that negatively impact on library customers and their experiences (e.g. vendors or suppliers that through ineffective service cause the library not to be able to deliver effective service, construction companies or other agencies that render the parking at or travel to the library inconvenient or difficult, etc.), as the customer usually does not distinguish between the library and the other organization or activity – it comes to the patron as all being interconnected to the library service experience;

- organizations and activities that render library communications processes about performance assessment information and evidence of service impact/value to customers, potential customers and stakeholders ineffective or inconsistent (e.g. library friends or support groups, smaller library units that do not support administrative communication of strategic decisions, community watchdog agencies or action groups and committees with political/social agendas that use perceived or unsubstantiated errors or conceptions of the library and its services to accomplish their goals, etc.);

- lastly the customer themselves – many customers would prefer to meet their own library and information service needs, just as they do in other aspects of their lives (i.e. having choices and control options like banking online, home delivery of resources and services, etc.).

The final competitive force in the library service environment is competition for resources. The competitors for resources are the most familiar to libraries, as they have encountered them for many years at local, regional and national levels of government and stakeholder group meetings. Here the most notable competitors in the library service environment are those that compete for customers' resources (i.e. access and time) and library staffing and financial resources.

The largest and most important resource in the library is people; the library staff and administrators who perform the work necessary to meet customers' library and information service needs and the customers who make the services of the library necessary and appreciated.

Libraries face competition from other service environment forces for the staff and administrators to operate the library and make the strategic decisions and resource allocations necessary to respond effectively to customer and stakeholder information needs. Many graduates of library and information science programs are hired into non-library work environments, especially by for-profit library service competitors like technology companies, internet services and retail bookstores. Library staff and administrators who have proven years of experience in lower-wage and lower-benefit positions leave library service provision for greater extrinsic rewards in for-profit competitors. These factors combine to make staffing and administration more difficult for library leaders and stakeholders. The library can only be competitive when the proper human resources (i.e. staff and administration) are dependably available to undertake essential library professional responsibilities, make strategic decisions and allocate resources effectively.

Customers and potential customers can only access the library services when they have time to do so, whether in person in the library or via electronic access. As research shows that more people are sleep-deprived from attempting or being required to achieve so much in a day, as family lives become more complicated with distance and time demands and as the number of avenues for customers' access continues to grow, the library not only has to fight to obtain new customers but is required to fight to keep existing customers. It is not only fighting to keep a customer, but fighting through the activity of life even to have a place in the customer's calendar. If the customer, no matter how enthused with the library and its services, cannot find the time to access the library or benefit from its services, a customer relationship gap is created and the library loses the customer (even if just temporarily). The library never really even gets to compete for the customer's business directly through its services and resources, as the customer cannot interact with the library. When this customer access gap occurs, customers lose some of their connection to the library, making them vulnerable to other service competitors' efforts and potentially less interested in supporting library staffing (i.e. volunteering), financial and other resource needs.

As with many other non-profit and governmental agencies, the library is struggling against increased needs for service and fewer resources available to provide those services. Libraries are seldom identified by their governing authorities or community leaders as mandated services (i.e. public services that must be provided by law to maintain the community's safety and security); thus when resources are threatened or reduced, non-mandated services like the library are usually the first to feel the cuts so that the governing authority can provide the mandated services.

Philanthropy has also become a more competitive process for libraries as they compete against universities, public health services and other social/educational organizations for financial resources. Libraries are experiencing this indirect competition for financial resources from other libraries and non-profits in identifying and obtaining alternative financial sources (i.e. grants, foundation funds, etc.), as more non-profit and library agencies are increasingly dependent on these alternative funds for survival.

Listed below are some examples of the competitors for resources faced by libraries.

■ Realities of customers' lives restrict their access to the library's services and resources in a busy world that is frequently short of time (work, family commitments, recreation alternatives, social service requirements, etc.). If the library's customers are too busy to access its services and resources, whether that customer was lost to another service provider or not, that customer is not using the library.

- Governing authorities or other organizations can impose legal restrictions or influence resource allocations (e.g. tax revenue restrictions, service area definitions, allocation formulas, etc.). This can prohibit the library from effectively and strategically serving customers or potential customers and prevent it from meeting service needs or growing its service environment.

- Other governmental and non-profit organizations are now competing for philanthropic and other alternative financial resources that libraries have traditionally depended on for support.

These visible and invisible competitors for library customers, while having various impacts on the service relationship between the library and its customers, potential customers and stakeholders, all have one thing in common: they prevent the library from being easy to do business with and create separations in the service relationship. If libraries are to be more competitive for customers in the future, they will need to respond to or reduce the competitive forces that create gaps in their customer service relationships. Libraries find it difficult enough to respond strategically to the service environment already; they do not need to expend extra efforts and resources repairing or re-establishing newly created gaps in their customer service relationships.

Challenges to obtaining competitors' information to make strategic decisions

The current competition being faced by libraries in their service environments is abundant in practice and evidence, however difficult to document. Traditionally, as library performance assessment has been primarily internally focused, there has been no historical record or assessment of the competition in the library's service environment. Currently, while there is some awareness of knowing more about the service environment than just what happens inside the library, most libraries do not gather assessment or comparative data on their competitors, so there is limited evidence to show the scope, scale or trends of competitive threats being experienced by libraries. Many of the competitive forces faced by libraries are indirect or invisible to library customers and staff, and are thus not documented well. Additionally, customers lost by libraries to other library and information service providers and competitors are frequently not identified, documented and researched to determine the reasons for their ending of the service relationship with the library.

On the part of the competitors for library service, their performance assessment and competitive information are not always readily available for public access. As some of the competition in the library's service environment is indirect or invisible, collecting information is even more difficult for libraries. However, through existing business reference and information resources, competitive intelligence, marketing analysis, demographics and other information collection and analysis processes, libraries can acquire and use performance data from competitors in developing strategic responses and making strategic decisions.

All these factors make it very difficult to determine the current issues connected to competition for library services and the possible successful strategies that libraries and library administrators could use in responding to the needs and service demands of their customers and stakeholders. Until more is known by library administrators and stakeholders about their service environments and their customers' and their own impacts and value creation, libraries will continue to struggle in their attempts to compete in their service environments.

Future needs

In the future, libraries will need to be able to document the forces at work in their service environment by transitioning the inward-focused, traditional performance assessment processes and metrics to include more external environmental data and information – more information from competitors. The lack of this documentation is directly responsible for the current lack of effective responses and knowledge available to library administrators and stakeholders to develop strategic responses to customer service needs.

The libraries of the future will need to work cooperatively to conduct performance assessments and gather critical competitive information as the blending of service environments, technologies, customers, organizational structures and resources continues. Most libraries will not be able to allocate the resources, technologies or time away from service delivery to gather the kinds of information to address the comprehensive data needs of library administrators to make effective strategic decisions, so cooperation to share effort and reduce resources in conducting performance assessments will be essential.

For those who doubt this can be done or that there is a value to this performance and competitive information, the author would refer the reader to the performance data collection and analysis systems of Wal-Mart and FedEx, which have been frequently documented in the business press. These companies value and depend on the performance and competitive information from their service environments for their strategic responses and decisions so much that they routinely invest millions of dollars a year in maintaining and innovating their assessment and competitive processes to ensure they are performing at their best.

Wal-Mart has the ability to record every aspect of every customer transaction (from both customer and store perspectives) worldwide and store it for two years while it is researched and analyzed for competitive information and trends in the service environment. Wal-Mart collects competitive and performance data from every vendor, sales contact, inventory and financial transaction, and customer interaction information is available usually within one hour to decision-making employees throughout all of Wal-Mart's 5,000+ store locations, supply centers and administrative units.

FedEx uses the latest technology to collect and analyze competitive and performance data automatically on approximately 100 performance indicators from all its stores, customers, suppliers/vendors and shipping centers worldwide. The results are compiled, analyzed and disseminated to FedEx executives every business day within hours of conducting its performance assessment processes. Executives then have almost real-time performance data from any location or any strategic aspect of their service environment to help them make strategic decisions, allocate resources or correct existing strategic decisions or strategies to ensure that their organization is effective in meeting customers' service needs and delivering all of the value to the customer that is created by FedEx.

In addition to the competitive benefits gained from using the results of the performance assessment process in developing strategic decisions and responses, FedEx is able to use the same logistical and performance information to add value to its customers' service experience. FedEx allows customers to access performance and other logistical information as part of their choices and experience, giving them more awareness and 'control' over what they know and when they know it. This information access provides the customer with self-mediated service and early warnings of problems in the service experience, which allow the customer to generate corrections and resolutions faster, thus providing additional value.

Wal-Mart and FedEx are just two of the highly competitive and successful organizations in the information service economy that use performance assessment and competitive information processes to make strategic decisions and generate strategic responses for their current and future service environments. Libraries cannot afford to ignore this competitive resource and must have this level of information to make strategic decisions and allocate resources, given the level of competition in their service environments and the advantage received from the efforts.

Identifying your competitors' service environment impacts

This chapter has identified the most common competitors in the library service environment, and discussed the issues, needs and value in obtaining performance data from this environment and the need to expand the understanding of the environment. Identifying the library and its competitors' service environment impacts and values is an integral part of a new, innovative library performance assessment process that will enable the library to make effective strategic decisions and allocate resources (i.e. develop strategic responses).

But how does this happen? What kinds of information should the library know about its service environment?

Figure 3.1 How does the library develop strategic responses?

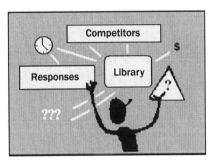

What kinds of information does the library need to know in order to generate effective strategic responses (Figure 3.1)? The answers to these and other questions related to the 'knowing' of the library service environment will be explained in Chapter 4.

4

Know things first: identifying strategic information needs

Traditional performance assessment and measurement have not provided libraries with the kinds of competitive information they need to know about their service environment. As explored in the previous chapters, library performance assessment and measurement have a variety of challenges that directly impact on how libraries report their value and performance to customers and stakeholders. Lack of resources, consistency, meaning and involvement by those outside the library in the assessment process have limited the benefit of performance assessment. These challenges, and a lack of understanding about the broader community within which the library operates, are leaving libraries in a position where they need to learn or know a great deal more about themselves, the people or communities they serve or impact and the competition in their service environment in order to be successful or maintain their existence or viability.

As competition for library and information services has increased, there is a growing competitive need for libraries to identify and know their own and competitors' service environment impacts and values. Service environment knowledge is an integral component of an innovative library performance assessment and competitive information process that is needed in order for the library to know how to generate strategic decisions and responses and improve its service environment impact and values.

Knowing what aspects of its existing services provide impact, value and greater access or control benefits and values to the customer, the library can use this information to understand better the customers and stakeholders it serves and create strategic responses that are more aligned to customer need. This should result in a more connected and supporting customer for the library and enhance the value of the results of the library's strategic development process. But the answers to these questions are not the only 'knowns' the library should have when developing strategic responses for its service environment.

What do you know about what your customers know?

Libraries have traditionally recorded the transactions of service in their assessment or performance measurement processes. These have included such measures as numbers of circulation, library visitors and dollars expended on service delivery or resource provision. But these performance data do not reveal the types of information that libraries now need know in order effectively to implement strategic responses that make a positive impact in the community. Understanding the library's multiple stakeholders' use or non-use of the library and other services in the service environment, what attracts customers to the library or its services and how customers benefit from the library and its services are the new types of data that libraries need to know in order to respond most effectively to customer and stakeholder needs.

Traditionally libraries have involved customers in very few of the performance assessment or competitive information processes. While asked by many libraries about what they like or do not like and what they need, overall customers and stakeholders are not a routine part of the performance or competitive information review. They are not involved in the process design or implementation, but are used as data sources (and only then for library inwardly focused issues) after the process has already been designed. They are usually not involved in analyzing the findings of performance assessment or competitive information processes, and may not always even receive the results of the processes when concluded. This has been an unfortunate practice by many libraries that will need to be resolved immediately if the library is to obtain the critical information and data it needs to make strategic decisions and implement effective services.

Library customers are a wealth of information for a library seeking to understand the meaning of this sometimes hidden resource and utilize this understanding in developing or assessing strategic responses. Not only can the customers share their insight about the library, its services and the desired/actual benefits, but they can provide the library with insight and information about other aspects of the service environment that it would not understand or have access to in other ways. For example, customers can share their experiences with:

- other services in the environment that they enjoy or benefit from using;
- other services in the environment that they do not enjoy or benefit from using;
- other library and information service providers in the environment that they enjoy or benefit from using;
- other library and information service providers in the environment that they do not enjoy or benefit from using;

- the services and received benefits from the library's competitors in the environment;

- new or pending trends, services, benefits or values being provided by library competitors in the service environment;

- new or pending trends, needs and developments in the services provided in the environment;

- gaps in services provided in the environment;

- gaps in benefits, values and impacts in the service environment;

- potential partners, collaborators and new customers in the service environment;

- feedback on potential strategic responses and impacts before implementation for refinement and support;

- new markets for existing services of the library.

Knowing this kind of performance and competitive information would be very beneficial to libraries. Understanding these data will provide a wealth of information to use in developing strategic responses and determining the effectiveness of or need for existing library strategic responses and services. Besides the direct value in understanding this information, the library would also benefit in that much of this information would not be possible to obtain from other sources without an extensive commitment of resources (i.e. staff time, skills, finances, etc.). Many of the library's customers are very willing to share this information with the library if asked in a concise and effective manner; they also freely provide it through suggestions in strongly positive/negative or unsatisfactory service experiences and through inquiries in seeking options or assistance filling a service need in the current services provided by the library.

Inviting customers to share these types of information with the library also creates a value-added relationship for the customer. The communication between the customer and the library in this exchange often creates a closer relationship and appreciation between the customer and the library, which can lead to greater support in future strategic developments and responses and lead customers to perceive greater benefit, impact or value in their service relationship with the library. All of these 'knowns' help the library to understand its service environment and develop more effective strategic responses. However, there are other stakeholders in the service environment that can help the library in this process; one is the library's competitors.

What do you know about your competitors?

Why should the library know more about its competitors? Besides being in the information business, libraries are also in the service business, and that means competition for services. The competition may be direct and next door to the library or indirect and miles away. Having a more complete understanding of the library's competitors (regardless of their size, location or directness) and their services/ customers is critical in this competitive service environment, as any competitor has the ability to impact on the library's service environment and therefore on the library in its strategic efforts and developments.

Traditionally, performance assessment and environmental scanning are the only information-gathering practices that libraries have used to understand their service environment. Performance assessment has almost always been inwardly focused on the library (i.e. excluding competitors) and environmental scanning is most commonly practiced as a passive effort, frequently missing competitor information that requires a more active (i.e. competitive intelligence or CI) effort and resources to obtain. So many libraries have little understanding of their competitors or their customers and are competing in a negative, reactive position in their own service environment because of this lack of understanding.

The types of information and understanding that the library could obtain from its competitors, its competitors' customers or its own customers include:

- other services in the library service environment that they enjoy or benefit from using;
- other services in the environment that they do not enjoy or benefit from using;
- other library and information service providers in the environment that they enjoy or benefit from using;
- other library and information service providers in the environment that they do not enjoy or benefit from using;
- the services and received benefits from the library's competitors in the environment;
- new or pending trends, services, benefits or values being provided by library competitors in the service environment;
- gaps in services provided in the service environment;
- gaps in benefits, values and impacts in the service environment;
- potential partners, collaborators and new customers in the service environment;
- feedback on potential strategic responses and impacts before implementation for refinement and support;
- new markets for existing services of the library.

Many of these are similar to the types of information gathered from the library's customers and can serve as a validity check against the customers' perceptions and information, thus creating more valid/credible information to make strategic decisions. The benefits to the library in knowing more about its competitors include learning about service innovations, knowing what services the library can offer to compete or respond to competition and recruiting new customers from competitors and new partners or collaborators in strategic response development and deployment.

Connecting the 'knowns'

The most effective approach for a library to identify and know the information about its service environment is to have a model for action in identifying and obtaining performance and competitive data and information. Unorganized activities to glean information from the service environment will not yield a complete and accurate picture of the environment and its needs. The model of action should describe what the library needs to know about the service environment; the sources of this information; what the possible uses of this information to generate strategic responses or decisions could be; how to determine the most effective strategic responses; and what potential impacts or values will be created with the known information. Once this model of action has been completed, the library will be able to use it in its strategic planning process to turn the service environment information into results, impacts and value for its customers and stakeholders.

The author has developed a model (Figure 4.1) that demonstrates how such a process to identify and know

Figure 4.1 White's strategic response development model

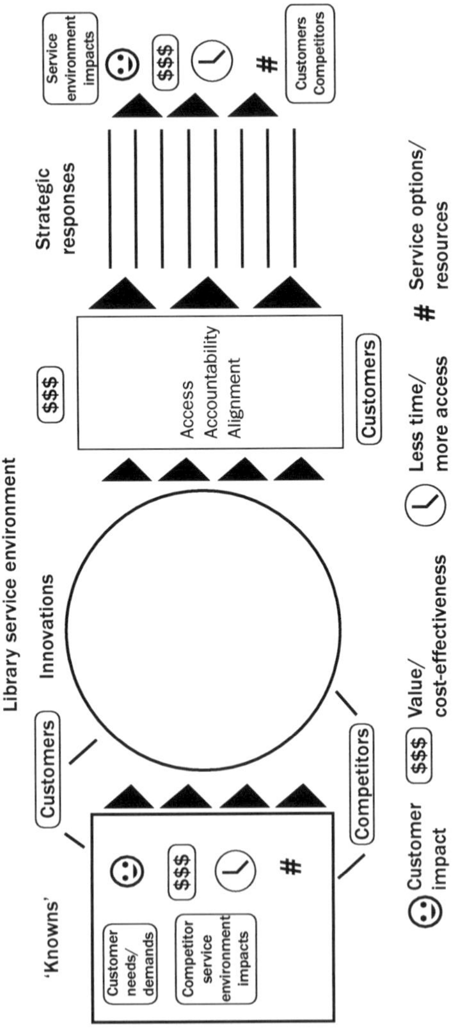

service environment information and generate strategic responses can be accomplished.

The model in Figure 4.1 depicts the library service environment and how the library can identify environmental information and transform it into potential strategic responses. The model has four components: 'knowns', 'innovations', 'AAA' and 'strategic responses'. Each component contains critical action and decision-making activities to help the library (staff, administrators and stakeholders) obtain, understand and process service environment information into potentially effective strategic decisions and responses. These four components work together within the library and between the library and its environment to accomplish the information collection and strategic response generation processes and ensure involvement from all members of the library's service environment.

The first component of the model is the 'knowns', highlighted in Figure 4.2. This component is called the 'knowns' because it identifies what the library 'knows' or needs to 'know' about its service environment (i.e. customers, stakeholders and competitors) and itself. The library must ensure that the 'knowns' component is effectively completed in order to ensure success in terms of identifying the information known and needed by the library and the sources of the needed information. Accurate evidence and information are essential to the overall success and effectiveness of the model: if the library does not have accurate and complete information about its service environment and itself, it will not generate the most effective strategic decisions and responses that will create the greatest amounts of impact and value for the library. The author has provided a series of template forms (see Appendix) for libraries to use in gathering and organizing the information

Figure 4.2 'Knowns' for developing strategic responses

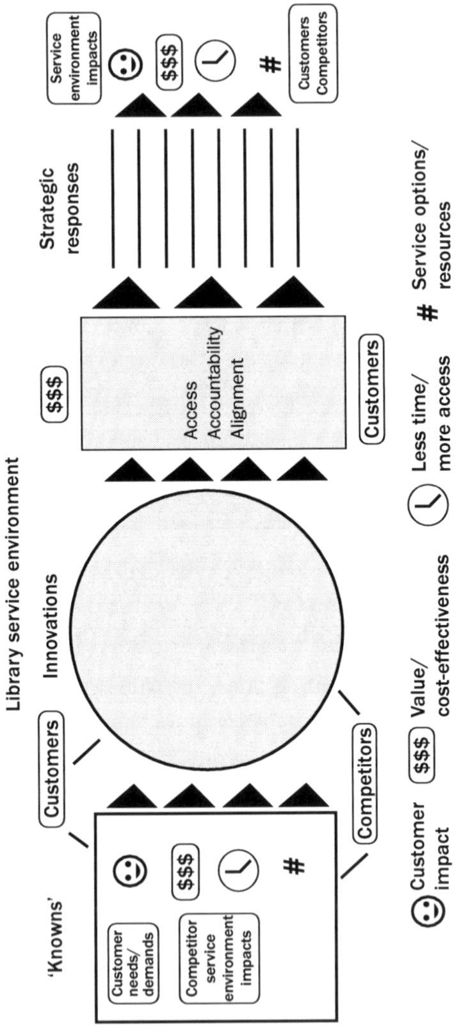

obtained about their service environment when developing strategic responses. The 'knowns' form can be found on page 109.

In the 'knowns' component of the model, the library will need to obtain evidence and information from five different sources: customers, stakeholders, service environment competitors, the service environment itself and the library itself. Each of these information sources has different perspectives, data and understanding about the library's service environment that is important for the library to know. While some of the data and understanding are openly/ publicly available, much is not unless the library actively identifies the sources and seeks out the information. The data and understanding from these five sources may also be conflicting and unverified; the library must make every effort to use only factual evidence and information that can be sourced and vetted to ensure that information used to make decisions is the most accurate and complete available.

In Tables 4.1–4.5, the 'knowns' sample question information matrices, the five information sources are aligned in a matrix against the categories of information the library needs to know. It is important to note that a listing of every question or type of information possibly needed under each information source is not conceivable for every library service environment or for these matrices; however, a brief listing of the most common or critical types of information needed to be known from each source is included to get started in the process. The scope of the answers and the resources of each library to address these questions will vary, and should be aligned to the appropriate level of response and resource by the library. All the sample questions need not be addressed at one time, nor do the answers require a dissertation to address them adequately. However, the answers should be as accurate and factually based as possible.

The five major stakeholders in the library service environment (customers, stakeholders, competitors, non-library users and the library itself) are asked to provide information in response to questions that explore the multiple perceptions of services needed. Note that the questions do not specifically focus on library or information services only. These more open questions will help respondents think about a wider set of services they may need, allow those without an expert understanding of the library and its services to respond comfortably and provide more innovative options for the library to explore in its strategic development process. Forcing respondents to view the world only through a set of library service needs confines their ability to respond effectively to the questions and creates an artificial barrier between the information known by the stakeholder (i.e. the source of strategic response development) and the library which needs to know and understand that information. It also restricts the library's ability to understand the service needs and their sources in the service environment and how it can effectively respond or create responses to these perceptions of needs. This is a critical point, as many libraries are now exploring the possibilities of providing (or being required by stakeholders to provide) more non-traditional information services as part of their mission and strategic responses or in response to competitive forces.

In obtaining responses from stakeholders, the library can and should employ options of gathering evidence from within and outside the library itself and within all aspects of the library service environment. Having an accurate understanding of these multiple perceptions of service needs is critical to the library in its strategic response development process. There are multiple stakeholder perceptions of the library performing these services, and how well the library meets these service needs will shape how each stakeholder group determines the library's service impact and value. If this information is not accurate or does not include these multiple perspectives, the rest of the strategy development process will be misaligned and will not yield the best results for the library's efforts. The library's strategic responses will not be wide enough in scope, prove effective in implementation or assessment, nor create the intended value for stakeholders, thus wasting library resources and community capital.

As one can see in Table 4.1, the questions are aimed at probing into what is known by the various library service environment stakeholders in regards to their perceptions of the service needs of the community. Table 4.1 also explores the stakeholders' perceptions of not only what services they perceive they need, but the factors each stakeholder associates with how the needed services should be provided and how they will benefit best from these services. These factors include the stakeholders' perceptions of who should provide the needed services and who is the best provider of the services. This is beneficial for the library to know: if the stakeholder perceives that the library is not the appropriate service provider, then pursuing the provision of that service need is not in a library's best interest as the stakeholder will doubt whether the need is effectively met because the library is not the appropriate provider. Knowing what your stakeholders do not expect from you is sometimes more valuable than knowing what they do expect, especially in a time of reduced resources and non-competitive opportunities. After all, the strategy of trying to be everything to everyone in the community is a flawed response, as it usually leads to the library performing a lot of routine services that are not especially innovative, nor used or valued by stakeholders. The results of this strategy usually give stakeholders the perception of the library being disconnected from the community and not making a difference in the community in spite of its efforts.

| Table 4.1 | 'Knowns' service needs/demands sample questions information matrix |

What does the library know about...?	Customer information	Stakeholder information	Competitor information	Service environment information (non-library users)	Library information
Service needs/ demands	What services are needed? Why are they needed? When are they needed? Do you think the library is the best provider to meet these needs? Do you need the library to provide these services?	What services are needed? Why are they needed? When are they needed? Do you think the library is the best provider to meet these service needs? Do you need the library to provide these services? Do you want the library to provide these services?	What services are provided? Who provides these needed services? Why are they provided? When are they provided? Who uses these services? How do they use these services? Who do you think is the best in meeting service needs? Do you know that the library provides these services?	What services are needed? Why are they needed? When are they needed? Who uses these needed services? How do they use these needed services? Who should meet the service needs? Do you think the library is the best provider to meet these needs? Do you need the library to provide these services?	What services are provided? Why are they provided? When are they provided? Do you think the library should be the best provider in meeting service needs? Do you want the library to provide these services?

Knowing the impact of service in the library environment (Table 4.2) is critical to the strategic response development process, as implementing services with no perceived benefit

Table 4.2	'Knowns' service impacts sample questions information matrix

What does the library know about...?	Customer information	Stakeholder information	Competitor information	Service environment information (non-library users)	Library information
Service impacts	What should library services do for you? What services/ resources are not making your life better? What services/ resources are making your life better? What difference is the library making to you? What difference do you most need the library to make to you?	What should library services do for the community? What library services/ resources are not making life better? What library services/ resources are making life better? What difference do you want the library to make? What is the most important difference the library can make?	What do your services do for the community? Which of your services/ products are not being used a lot? Which of your services/ products are making the community better? What difference could collaborating with the library make to you?	What should these services do for the community? What services/ resources are not making the community better? What services/ resources are making the community better? What difference can the library make in the community? What difference do you most need the library to make in the community?	What should your library's services do for the community? What library services/ resources are not making the community better? What library services/ resources are making your life better? What difference can the library make to the community?

to any stakeholder group is an ineffective strategic response. Understanding the multiple perspectives of the impact of library and other services ensures that the library's existing strategic responses are creating a positive impact for stakeholders and that newly developed strategic responses are aligned to maximize their impact on the library's service environment.

Knowing the impacts of both library and other services in the service environment is critical to the library's understanding of its strategic options and responses. In our competitive service environments, turning non-users into customers or stakeholders who value and support the library is an essential survival tactic. While we would like to think that the library is one of only a few organizations that positively impact on the community, in fact many organizations actually do so. In exploring the multiple perspectives of the impact of library and other services in its service environment, the library can learn the overall trends and developments in services and service delivery, the gaps in service impact that might be exploited by the library, the types and extent of the impact created by services and the essential elements of how each stakeholder group benefits from the services provided. Knowing this will allow the library to create services that most align with the perceived needs of the library's environment and stakeholders, thus ensuring a more effective strategic response. This is especially true when developing responses for the non-library users. If you do not know what affects these elusive stakeholders, you cannot develop effective strategic responses that will entice their use or valuation of the library, nor will their perceptions of a wider community impact from the library-provided services be transitioned to a positive position in support of the library.

Knowing the value derived from services in the library environment (Table 4.3) is critical to developing new strategic responses or reaffirming existing responses. Strategic responses that do not create value for library stakeholders are strategic failures, even if implemented

Table 4.3 'Knowns' value from service sample questions information matrix

What does the library know about...?	Customer information	Stakeholder information	Competitor information	Service environment information (non-library users)	Library information
Value from service	What library services provide you with the most value? Why? What library services provide you with the least value? Why? What value do you need the library to provide that you are not receiving now? Why? What service values are most important to you? Why?	What library services provide you with the most value? Why? What library services provide you with the least value? Why? What value do you need the library to provide that you are not receiving now? Why? What service values are most important to you? Why?	What services do you provide that generate the most value for your customers? How do you know that? What services do you provide that generate the least value? How do you know that? What service values do you believe need to be provided to the community that it is not receiving now? Why? What service values are most important to you? Why?	What services provide you with the most value? Why? What services provide you with the least value? Why? What service values do you need the library to provide that you are not receiving now? Why? What service values are most important to you? Why?	What library services provided by the library offer the community the most value? Why do you think this? What services provided by the library offer the community the least value? Why? What service values does the library need to provide that you are not providing now? Why? What service values are most important to you? Why?

71

perfectly and requiring no resources, as they do not create the long-term or broad stakeholder/community support and evidence of community impact that the library needs to maintain its viability and competitive position in the service environment.

The library can benefit in many ways from knowing information about service value in its environment. Eliminating strategic responses that do not generate a positive community value (whether in financial, political, social, etc. terms and measures) can reduce or eliminate the self-induced strategic obstacles created in its environment that the library will need to overcome. The elimination of negative-value-creation responses will either cease the creation of negative-impact perceptions or increase stakeholder perceptions of the library's value to the community. It also frees up library resources and opportunities that can generate the necessary long-term and broad stakeholder support and value needed by the library. This in turn provides more effective value creation by the library and its strategic responses by generating new, potentially positive values/impacts in the library environment.

Knowing what services provide the multiple stakeholder groups with the greatest access to the library's services, and therefore create a positive impact, is of interest to a library when developing strategic responses (Table 4.4). If the stakeholders cannot access the library's services or facilities, they cannot experience, value or support those services. If the library understands how the multiple stakeholder groups are currently hindered in access or benefiting from access to the library and its services, the library can use that understanding to develop new strategic responses that either remove hindrances or enhance existing benefits, creating an added impact within the library service environment.

Table 4.4 'Knowns' service access/time savings sample questions information matrix

What does the library know about...?	Customer information	Stakeholder information	Competitor information	Service environment information (non-library users)	Library information
Service access/ time savings	What library services do you have access to? What library services save you time? Why? What library services provide you with the most access to what you need from the library? Why? What access to the library or its services do you need the library to provide that you are not receiving now? Why? What access to the library or its services is most important to you? Why?	What library services do you have access to? What library services save you time? Why? What library services provide you with the most access to what you need from the library? Why? What access to the library or its services do you need the library to provide that you are not receiving now? Why? What access to the library or its services is most important to you? Why?	What services of yours do your customers have access to? What types of services save you time? Why? What services provide your customers with the most access to what they need from you? Why? What access to your services do your customers need you to provide that you are not providing now? Why? What access to your services is most important to your customers? Why?	What information services do you have access to? What information services save you time? Why? What information services provide you with the most access to what you need? Why? What access to information services do you need provided that you are not receiving now? Why? What access to information services is the most important to you? Why?	What library services can you not provide access to? What library services save you time? Why? What access to the library or its services do you know needs to be provided to customers that you are not providing now? Why? What access to the library or its services is most important to your customers? Why?

73

Effective access to library services and facilities is often taken by customers as meaning quick or convenient access that saves them time. Time is viewed by many as a highly precious resource in today's hectic life. Anything that saves time for someone is often viewed as having a great deal of value. If the library knew what aspects of its services were perceived by customers and stakeholders as time savers, (i.e. customer/community value), then it could develop new services (i.e. value) for customers by reducing the customer's time involved in accessing the service or increasing the time the customer has access to the service.

Aligning existing or new strategic responses and services to create the added value of convenience or time savings is often a positive impact for the customer and a resource saving to the library. One method used to help align strategic responses and services to customers' needs or benefits is to provide customers with resources to support or enhance their access to the library and its services (i.e. benefit or value) or access to the service process to allow customers to self-mediate the service to their benefit.

Providing customers with the options and resources to mediate their access (i.e. benefit and value) gives a more intimate service experience and allows the benefits of the service to be experienced at a more personal level of connection, thus any impact generated (hopefully positive in nature) connects more strongly to the customer. Many businesses and non-profit organizations benefit from providing this increased access or customer control in their service provision. The development of resources and services that allow customers some control over their service experiences – for example online banking, grocery delivery, ordering merchandise, answering questions or donations to charities or other groups – has increased customer appreciation and created new customers for the organizations that provide

Table 4.5 'Knowns' service options/resources sample questions information matrix

What does the library know about...?	Customer information	Stakeholder information	Competitor information	Service environment information (non-library users)	Library information
Service options/ service resources	What service options do you need to enhance the value gained from the services you receive? What options or resources do you need to enhance the value you receive from library services? What library service options or resources available at present provide you with the most value? Why? What library service options or resources available at present do you wish you had more choices in or control over? Why?	What service options do you need to enhance the value gained from the services you receive? What options or resources do you need to enhance the value you receive from library services? What library service options or resources available at present provide you with the most value? Why? What library service options or resources available at present do you wish you had more choices in or control over? Why?	What service options do your customers request to enhance the value they receive from your services? What options or resources do you provide to customers to enhance the value they receive from you? What service options or resources available to your customers at present provide them with the most value? Why? What library service options or resources available to your customers at present do they request more choices in or control over? Why?	What service options do you need to enhance the value gained from the services you receive? What options or resources do you need to enhance the value you receive from information services? What information service options or resources available at present provide you with the most value? Why? What information service options or resources available at present do you wish you had more choices in or control over? Why?	What service options can you provide to enhance the value customers receive from your resources? What options or resources do you need to enhance to provide more value from library services? What service options or resources available to customers at present provide them with the most value? Why? What service options or resources do customers request more choices in or control over? Why?

75

them. While some libraries currently incorporate this practice, libraries as whole may need to examine this perceived need by customers and non-customers to enhance their competitive presence in their service environment (Table 4.5).

Once these knowns and any other types of information are obtained by the library, the next step in the process of developing strategic responses is to take the information and understanding thus obtained and to use it in developing effective responses. Chapter 5 will explain how the library can begin transforming its knowns into strategic actions through innovation.

5

'Knowns' are really verbs: using innovation to transform the 'knowns' into potential strategic responses

After obtaining performance and competitive information and data from the assessment and information-gathering processes, the library needs to transform the understanding of this information into potential strategic options and responses to benefit fully from this process.

At the heart of the 'knowns' information and data are the service needs of the multiple customers and stakeholders within the library's service environment. The 'knowns' information includes cultural and demographic data, development plans, economic conditions, information sources, technologies and the performance of existing services and gaps within the services provided in the library. By analyzing and understanding this information, the library obtains beneficial and critical strategic information on which to base future planning and decision-making:

- customer, stakeholder, competitor and service environment impacts (negative impacts to prevent and positive impacts to generate);

- customer, stakeholder, competitor and service environment values (negative values to reduce/eliminate and positive values to generate) and effectiveness (perceptions of current effectiveness, how defined, and future expectations);

- refinements of current provision that reduce service times experienced by customers and stakeholders or expand access to existing services;

- potential service options and resources that will enhance existing services or add value to future service provision when included in implementation.

Libraries are often identified or perceived as being warehouses of information; this is frequently true of information the library knows about itself. Many libraries have collections of known data and information about the library and its performance stored in ring-binders or other formats that line administrative office shelves and filing cabinets. The data and information within these unused locations generate no strategic benefit unless acted upon by the library. This unused (and therefore non-beneficial) information is called 'orphaned data and knowledge' (ODK), which is defined as 'data and knowledge generated by an organization that is inaccurate, misinterpreted, unnecessary, under-appreciated, under-accessed, or under-used and therefore does not provide recipients with the intended or potential value of the data or information' (White, 2002: 284). Besides the cost of obtaining such data and information, the library bears the costs of storing and maintaining the ODK while losing out on their potential strategic benefits; a costly process in multiple ways for a library that does not use its known data and information. The library can use this beneficial understanding to begin to identify potential innovations of service or service provision, but only if the 'knowns' information is acted upon or used. The 'knowns' information conveys the need of action or use to the competitive library, thus the 'knowns' become verbs to realize their true benefit and value to the library in the strategic response development process.

How does the library act upon or use the 'knowns' data and information to generate innovation, which is the start of strategic response development? By continually innovating its services and service delivery processes. But why should the library continue innovating these processes?

As depicted in Figure 5.1, the need for innovation within the service environment is dictated by the use of innovation throughout the library's service environment – which is not static. It is a dynamic environment that is always experiencing change and innovation:

- customers' perceptions and needs change and expand;

- stakeholders' expectations change and expand;

- the library's competitors are changing and expanding their services to compete against others (i.e. the library);

- resources and their availability/quality change;

- technology expedites wider access and faster services than before;

- the need to grow the library and its customer base for support and viability continues to expand.

The competitive library needs to innovate to respond, if not drive, the competitive service environment in which it finds itself. First, if the library did what it currently does 100 per cent effectively (which is nearly impossible, but suppose it could) at present and never changed, it would seem to customers and stakeholders to be antiquated and disconnected from the community as the rest of the community continued to expand and experience the innovation and changes that naturally occur. Secondly, the library's customers, regardless of their dedication to the library, are always seeking out the

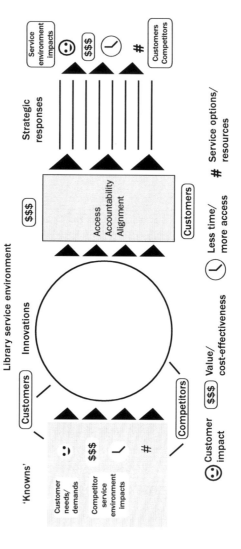

Figure 5.1 Innovations in strategic response development

latest, greatest or new items, services, programs, etc. It is these innovations that hold their interest and keep them coming back and not going somewhere else for their information service needs. Lastly, innovation stops the library and its staff from becoming complacent and reactive, which are two of the key ingredients for strategic failure and organizational decay.

There are many sources of innovation for the library to use in creating potential strategic responses from the 'knowns' data and information. As previously stated, the library's customers, staff, competitors and stakeholders are key sources of information for potential innovations of service and service delivery processes (even if you cannot innovate the service, if you innovate the delivery process you innovate the service and its impact on the service environment). However, there are other important sources of innovation that the library should be aware of and use when possible and appropriate:

- innovations in ideas (how people perceive and understand their environment);
- innovations from non-customers or non-stakeholders;
- innovations from technology;
- innovations in assessment and competitive processes.

Innovation from ideas

Innovations from ideas come as changes or expansions of how people perceive and understand their environment and needs occur. Each generation creates new experiences and perceptions of how their community works, their role in the community and what they need to be successful or survive in their community. This creates new cultures, philosophies and economic/political realities that in turn affect the community as a whole.

The 'knowns' data and information can gather this type of innovation resource for the library by examining the current and potential cultures, philosophies and economic/political realities of customers, stakeholders and non-customers within the service environment. Identifying the corresponding service needs (especially the library and information services needs) of these customers, stakeholders and non-customers provides the library with insight into how existing and potential services can address these needs or be available when the needs occur. This allows the library to be perceived more as a proactive organization than a reactive body, and as an innovative component of the service environment. The sources of information on innovation within the ideas of the community include schools (all types), community centers, cultural centers, civic engagement locations, religious service centers, arts and entertainment centers, heritage centers, local media outlets, special population gathering points and government/ public service locations.

Innovation from non-customers/ stakeholders

Innovations from non-customers/stakeholders are often a hidden treasure for libraries to capture. By definition, these individuals or groups are not regularly interactive with the library, and thus obtaining their understanding of their needs and perceptions of services can be difficult for many libraries. However, libraries need to make the effort to capture this information whenever possible, as the perceptions of those from outside the library on its relationship to the service environment are very different and allow insight that is often blocked by familiarity. Each non-customer or non-stakeholder can provide both individual and group perceptions of why the library is not their primary library and information service provider. Knowing why they do not use your services or what they perceive that keeps them from using these services can provide unique perspectives that would not be experienced or reported by most library customers.

The 'knowns' data and information can gather this type of innovation resource for the library by identifying and engaging non-customers/stakeholders in examinations of their perceptions and experiences. The customers of competitors or other information services providers (whether libraries or organizations/businesses that supply similar services) are also excellent sources of innovation as they provide insight and experience from the library competitor's point of view. This gives the library information on current or future services and strategic response options that existing library customers/stakeholders could benefit from if implemented, and what services and strategic response options might lure non-customers/stakeholders to the library or persuade the competitor's customers/stakeholders to move to the library as their provider of services and impact. Sources of information on innovations from non-customers/stakeholders within the library service environment include library business information resources, governmental/oversight organizations, any organization or business in the service environment or serving the environment (i.e. via the internet) that offers similar services to the library, and other libraries and information providers.

Innovations from technology

Innovations from technology come almost every day, it seems. A new device with new capabilities, a new use for older technologies, new access to a previously unavailable service or resource; these are almost daily occurrences for the library service environment and the people who live in it. These technological innovations can make processes faster, cheaper and more accessible. They can introduce or lure new users of the technology. They can change how people think and experience services, and drive how people perceive their needs and how they need to be addressed. Each new innovation of technology creates new experiences and perceptions of how the community works and what is possible in this community. This technology innovation drives the innovation of ideas and the innovation of non-customers/stakeholders (especially those who view the library as not being technology-oriented or effective), two other major sources of innovation within the library environment, and therefore the corresponding perceptions and needs of the community, so it can have a multiplier effect on innovation. The sources of information on technological innovations within the community include technology schools and service centers, local electronics stores, technology interest groups and gathering centers, social groups that focus on new and emerging technologies, and children/teens/young adults/young at heart who are always searching out the cool new technologies and understand their use and impacts.

Innovation from assessment and competitive processes

Innovation from assessment and competitive information processes – is it possible? Not only is it possible, but it is necessary!

As covered in Chapter 2, innovation in the library's assessment and competitive processes allows it continuously to improve the scope, depth and benefit of the information and understanding of the information obtained through these processes. The 'knowns' data and information can gather this type of assessment and competitive innovation information for the library by examining its existing processes for effectiveness and scope in obtaining the appropriate data and information to address strategic decision-making and planning and any information/understanding gaps that may exist. The sources of innovation within the library's assessment and competitive information processes include the previously stated future needs in Chapter 2, identifying and understanding the effective competitive intelligence practices employed by other service/library and information service providers in the service environment, and the incorporation of the other innovation sources discussed (i.e. ideas, non-customers/stakeholders and technology) into the library's assessment processes.

So there are multiple sources of innovation available to the library to use in converting the 'knowns' into potential beneficial strategic responses. The library should identify the innovative resources within its service environment and examine the possibilities of innovation that can be used with the 'knowns' data and information to see how customer needs can be strategically addressed. The Appendix provides a template form for libraries to use in identifying potential innovations and possible sources of innovation using the 'known' information from their service environment. The 'innovations' form can be found on page 110.

Warning: don't innovate because you can

While it is in the best interest of the library to innovate its services and service delivery processes when generating effective strategic responses, if it innovated everything connected to the library and its services there would be some counterproductive and negative consequences. That is why it is important to understand the 'knowns' and what the information describes to the library before beginning the innovation process. The library should seek to maintain those existing services and service delivery methods that are generating positive service environment value and impact unless:

- the degree of increase in service value and impact of a possible innovation is greater than the resources necessary to generate the potential service;

- the current value and impact of the existing services are substantially below other providers in the library's service environment;

- there are strategic gaps in service or service delivery processes that could lure new customers or strategic opportunities for the library from competitors in the service environment;

- the library has the appropriate resources and knowledge to implement the new innovations effectively or can obtain the resources and knowledge to do so.

If the library cannot satisfactorily address these criteria, it should reconsider whether to implement the potential innovations in service or service delivery processes at a later time when it is more capable of doing so effectively. After all, it is better to have a delayed success than an on-time failure.

So how does the library know which potential strategic responses are the best to implement? Chapter 6 explores this process, and provides an overview of how the library can best determine the most effective strategic responses.

6

Improving potential strategic responses through access, accountability and alignment

This chapter explores how the library can examine the potential strategic responses developed from applying innovation to the 'knowns' data and information gathered from its service environment to identify those responses that will have the most effective strategic success for the library and generate the services that will allow customers to maximize the benefits/values of their relationship to the library in order to maximize positive community impact.

In the strategic development process so far, the library has collected a set of 'knowns' about its service environment that include the library's customers, stakeholders, competitors and non-customers in the information process. The 'knowns' information and data are analyzed and used by the library and the members of its service environment to:

- know and better understand the service environment;
- know and understand the library and information needs of the service environment;
- know and understand the value and service impacts most needed in the service environment;
- know which of these library and information needs of the service environment the library can be most effective in addressing.

The library processes this information, understanding and innovations into possible strategic responses that create potential positive impacts or values to address the needs of the service environment most effectively. The possible responses are then analyzed to determine if they increase the access to library services and benefits to the service environment, and create and demonstrate effective uses of library and environmental resources in their implementation.

If a strategic response has withstood all these analyses in the strategic development process so far, it now faces its toughest analysis to date in ensuring that the potential response aligns the library with the service environment in a positive or effective manner. Effectively aligning the potential strategic response is the most critical stage in the development process, as this is what most ensures that a response effectively addresses need while generating the most value and impact for the library, its customers/stakeholders and its service environment. Regardless of the quality and soundness of the process used by the library in developing potential strategic responses, if a response does not align well between the library and the service environment it will not be totally effective in addressing needs or creating value/impact, and thus the strategic response development process has yielded less than effective results.

One example of this can be found in the late 1970s in the automotive industry. Chevrolet had developed and introduced an affordable car called the 'Nova' in the North American market to address the need for a nice-looking, good-mileage car at a time of gas shortages in the USA. The Nova sold well in the USA for several years, so the leaders of Chevrolet decided that, as Mexico was experiencing a similar set of conditions, the Nova would sell well in Mexico too. Chevrolet introduced the car into the Mexican market with great fanfare, but after several months of marketing and efforts, the sales of the Nova were almost non-existent. So what was the problem?

The problems in the Nova sales process were all connected to the fact that Chevrolet had not made a significant effort to know about its potential new market (i.e. needs, culture, etc.) and had not aligned the Nova and its introduction to this market. Chevrolet did not effectively listen to what the local Mexican dealers told it about the problems and how to address them. If it had, Chevrolet would have realized that the car's name, Nova, when translated into Spanish became 'No va' or 'no go'. The car's name in Spanish indicated to potential buyers that it would not go, i.e. was broken or bad, and no one was rushing to buy a car that would not work. Even when the Nova was otherwise exactly what was wanted by the market, because the car and its introduction were not properly aligned, the result was less than impressive and costly for Chevrolet.

Another example of this alignment problem was the introduction of 'new' Coke by the Coca-Cola Company in 1985. As Pepsi was gaining market share and sales volume with its flagship product 'Pepsi-Cola' in the early 1980s in the USA, Coca-Cola began developing a new version of its product to compete with Pepsi. As Pepsi's cola was deemed to be a sweeter drink than Coke, New Coke was developed and marketed as being like Pepsi's cola in the hope of regaining some of the lost market share and sales that Pepsi had recently claimed. The introduction of New Coke became an instant failure for Coca-Cola.

As Coca-Cola had not aligned the New Coke product with its customer wants/needs and its product development process, New Coke disappointed existing customers and did not effectively create the product that Pepsi customers really wanted either, thus Coca-Cola failed in both efforts to capture its lost market share and sales. New Coke was pulled from shelves in stores and the 'old' Coke was reintroduced with great fanfare, and Coca-Cola regained its disappointed customers.

As one can see in these two examples, alignment is critical in the strategic development process, and has to be maintained throughout the development process to ensure the generation of the most effective strategic responses by the library. The process of obtaining the 'knowns' of the service environment, the identification and development of service innovations, and the intended benefits, values and impacts must all be aligned to connect the library to its environment in the most strategic and productive relationships and interactions to maximize success.

In short, the goal of the library in developing strategic responses is to improve or expand services to customers/stakeholders (i.e. access), make effective use of the resources provided by the community (i.e. accountability) and ensure that the services provided meet community needs and generate a positive impact in the service environment (i.e. alignment). So to ascertain whether a potential strategic response generated through the development process model will meet these three goals, the library should analyze the potential response to see if it effectively aligns to address these goals.

Returning to the strategic development model, Figure 6.1 shows how the potential strategic responses resulting from the innovation component of the model are directed into an analysis that focuses on increasing the value and/or cost-effectiveness of the responses while correspondingly aligning them with the needs of the library's customers, stakeholders and community within the service environment. This alignment analysis is done by focusing on the library's service environment in conjunction with three focal areas that strengthen the library's strategic relationships with this

Figure 6.1 Innovations and access, accountability and alignment in strategic response development

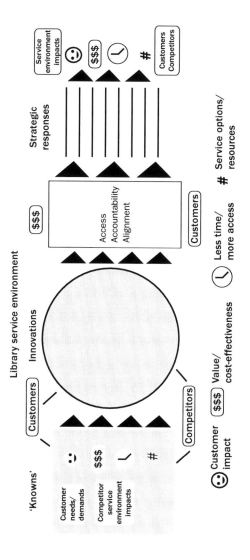

environment: access, accountability and alignment. The Appendix provides a template form for libraries to use when analyzing the areas of access, accountability and overall alignment (AAA) to improve the potential effectiveness of service innovations when developing strategic responses. The 'AAA' form can be found on page 112.

Strategic responses and access

Aligning a potential strategic response to create effective access to library services and benefits is done by analyzing how well the potential response either improves existing access or generates new access. If a potential strategic response does not increase access to library services or benefits, then it is not aligned with the library and community service environment needs and therefore it is not in the strategic interest of the library to pursue that response. There are many factors to consider when analyzing the alignment of access in a potential strategic response to the needs of the library's service environment.

The first consideration is whether the potential response is designed to address a short-term (i.e. less than a year) or a long-term (i.e. more than a year) strategic service environment need. The duration of the response should match the duration of the need. If the duration of the potential response exceeds that of the service environment needs, then the library is expending resources and strategic effort in excess of the need it was designed to address and thus the library is not strategically using its resources effectively in generating service and value for its customers and stakeholders. If the duration of the potential strategic response is short term and the service environment need is long term, then the potential response will not been seen or appreciated by customers, stakeholders and the service environment as having effectively responded to or addressed the need. Even if the potential response is implemented effectively and generates value, its short duration will leave an expectations gap between the library and its customers, stakeholders and service environment. This gap will be perceived as the library's service response not being effective in fully addressing the need for service. The end result is that the library will not fully benefit from the exerted strategic effort, and an increased future strategic effort will need to be made to overcome the expectations gap in addition to creating the intended service benefit and value to strengthen the relationship between the library and its service environment.

Another consideration in the alignment analysis of a potential strategic response is determining whether the response improves library customers' access to existing services and benefits; if existing customers do not perceive continued or expanded service provision and benefit and addressment of their needs, the library could lose customers to competing service providers. In this case, the strategic impact of the service in the service environment is diminished, as the numbers of recipients of the service and its benefits have been reduced, the library's ability to count on future support from customers is diminished and its future strategic responses will have to be even more effective to recoup the lost service environment impact. If the potential strategic response supports or expands services and benefits that existing customers perceive as being responsive and effective, then the library will not only retain its customer base but will continue to benefit from their support in the future.

Connected to the previous alignment analysis is how the strategic response expands future access to services and benefits for current, future and potential new customers of the library. The response should allow the library to build development capacity in service provision or delivery processes so that future enhancements or expansions of service are possible. Pursuing services, technologies or delivery processes that do not allow for flexible growth, adaptation and continued innovation are strategic responses with limited benefit to both the library and its service environment. The potential response should also allow the current services of the library to expand and adapt to increase the library's customer appeal and allow it to recruit new customers in the future. The library must have the ability to innovate its services (and therefore its benefits) continually to allow it to remain competitive and replace lost customers or recruit competitors' customers for long-term strategic success. A potential strategic response that limits future services and benefits, no matter how well implemented, is not a long-term success for the library or its service environment.

Another alignment analysis consideration is whether the potential strategic response reduces barriers to obtaining service (and therefore benefits or value) for existing customers (especially underserved locations/populations in the service environment) and future customers of the library. Even if the library could not expand or improve upon a service itself, the delivery of that service could be modified to reduce barriers to its use. For example, if the library cannot afford self-checkout machines to aid in speedier circulation of materials, reducing the time in line and reducing the physical barriers to accessing the library and its circulation service do increase access to the library's services and the benefits to the service environment. By making the library 'easier to do business with', library customers can save time in receiving and benefiting from its service and a wider scope of access is provided to the service environment; this widens the scope of benefit from the library to its environment, and thus increases service impact on the environment.

Strategic responses and accountability

Aligning a potential strategic response to enhance the library's ability to account effectively for its efforts, resource usage and generated impact for the service environment is a potent strategic success. Effectively demonstrating and reporting the strategic effort and value generated by the library for the service environment, reducing or justifying resource use in an effective stewardship process and providing positive service environment impacts through enhanced value and benefits from effective service are critical to the future competitiveness of the library. The library that can generate strategic responses which align accountability between the library and its service environment increases its competitiveness by reinforcing existing customer and stakeholder support, justifying existing and future resource allocations and defending the library (and its customers) from other competitors in the service environment, which all create future interest in and support for the library. If a potential response does not enhance the library's ability to account for its services, resources or impacts, then it is not aligned with the library and community service environment needs and thus it is not in the short- or long-term strategic interests of the library to pursue it.

There are several factors to consider when analyzing the alignment of accountability in a potential strategic response to the needs of the library's service environment. The first is whether the potential strategic response allows the library to report effectively its efforts in implementing the response. All successful responses will need to be measurable in terms of effort generated, service provided, resources used, quality of service, etc., or the library will not generate evidence it can use to address the accountability questions and issues its faces from its customers, stakeholders and the service environment. If the potential response is not measurable or if the library does not assess its success or effectiveness, then the library gains no strategic ability to justify its current strategic efforts, and therefore loses a strategic opportunity in the service environment to provide evidence of responsiveness and impact. This result reduces the library's ability to garner support from its customers and stakeholders in maintaining existing resources or in obtaining future or increased resources, which reduces its competitive ability in the service environment.

Another aspect of this alignment analysis is whether the potential strategic response reduces the use of existing resources or ensures the effective use of existing/future resources. If the library service or its delivery method is innovated and the library can conserve or recapture some of the resources used to implement or provide the services, it can reallocate those resources to supporting or enhancing other existing services or the creation of new services, and enhance strategic success possibilities in other aspects of its service environment. If customers, stakeholders and the service environment perceive the library as a good steward of resources, they will be more supportive of future or additional requests for resources for the library. The evidence of effective resource use and management is also a critical consideration for resource providers like granting agencies, foundations and other similar philanthropic bodies on which libraries depend to provide services to the service environment.

The last alignment analysis consideration of a potential strategic response is whether it will create greater current or future positive value and impact or give the strategic capacity for the library to do so when delivering services to customers and the service environment. There are several aspects of this alignment, all dealing with the future capacity or ability of the library to be increasingly accountable and competitive. One aspect is analyzing if the potential strategic response delivers greater existing or future positive value and impact to the library's current customers, stakeholders and service environment. If the response does not increase positive value and impact, but does reduce existing or future negative value and impacts for customers, stakeholders and the service environment, then it could also be viewed as effectively aligned in terms of accountability. Lastly, if the potential response generates strategic partnerships, collaborations and opportunities that would currently or in the future benefit the library, it would be effectively aligned in terms of accountability.

The alignment of the library's potential strategic responses to the access and accountability foci ensures that the overall effect of the potential responses generates as much strategic success and value for the library and its customers, stakeholders and service environment as is possible. By generating increased access to its service and benefits and greater evidence of accountability in effort and resource use, the library is perceived by its customers, stakeholders, competitors and service environment as being more capable and competitive. These perceptions result in several strategic benefits and beneficial options being created for the library's use:

- improved connections and strategic relationships between the library and its customers, stakeholders and service environment;

- perceptions of the library proactively, innovatively and effectively engaging and addressing the needs of its service environment, customers and stakeholders;

- strengthened support for the library by customers, stakeholders and the service environment in current and future situations of strategic or competitive challenges;

- expanded participation in the library's operations and services by customers, stakeholders, partners, collaborators, competitors and the service environment;

- improved communication between the library and its customers, stakeholders and the service environment on needs addressment and the value and impacts generated by the library and received by the service environment.

The library can use these benefits and beneficial options to enhance its own abilities in a multiplier effect, which increases the output of the strategic effort and maximizes strategic impact and value for everyone. As everyone wants to be part of a success, the library would have reduced obstacles in generating or attracting strategic resources and support to remain viable and competitive in its service environment.

So once the library has performed this strategic response development process and began generating strategically effective services that enhance impact and competitive ability for this year, the library is done, right? Not so fast, my friend!

This strategic response development is an ongoing process that is continually being performed by the library. Chapter 7 describes the need for this continuous effort in strategic response development and how the library can perform this effort effectively over time.

7

Wash. Rinse. Repeat. Strategic responses are an ongoing process

The library has now completed one round of the performance assessment and strategic response development process and has generated potentially effective responses and identified innovations that are required, and the potential impacts and values of these responses. The Appendix provides a template form for libraries to use when compiling the results of the strategic response development process model and planning the actions to implement responses (the 'strategic response compilation' form can be found on page 114). The library's job is done now, right?

It is never done.

Really!

This can be illustrated with the following analogy. If you have ever read the instructions for using hair shampoo, they usually require the customer to wash their hair with generous amounts of shampoo, rinse out the shampoo and then repeat the process until satisfied with the results. While seeming simple and good-natured enough, this set of directions is quietly leading the customer to use a lot of shampoo and a lot of effort to be satisfied with the results (i.e. clean hair). This process does not end, though; as you have gotten used to clean hair, you do not hesitate to continue to use the shampoo and receive the benefits of clean hair. If you stop using lots of shampoo and effort, the results go away quickly and your unwashed hair returns.

Just as the hair shampoo and its results are washed away, the same is true with the performance assessment and strategic response development processes; once begun, you need to continue to use them to continue realizing their benefits. Otherwise, all of the shampoo (i.e. resource and effort) goes down the drain and the problem (i.e. strategic challenges and competition) returns.

After all, the library has invested a lot of resources into assessing its performance, learning about its competitive environment, identifying service needs, developing innovations in service and delivery to provide services to its environment and aligning these innovations to the service environment to increase access and enhance accountability in order to create strategic value and impact for the library. These efforts and resources have generated new services and potential long-term strategic benefits, values and impacts for the library that would then lose momentum without continued efforts and resources.

So stopping the strategic response development and performance assessment processes after one routine would effectively end the generation of strategic impact and value for the library and provide the perceptions of wasted effort and resources in the eyes of customers, stakeholders and the service environment. The library would no longer be perceived as proactive and responsive to the needs of its environment and would begin to erode what existing strategic success and impacts it possesses, making it more difficult in the next effort to overcome and be successful in strategic response development. Libraries that have difficulty in developing effective strategic responses will experience the eventual decay, decline and departure of the library in its service environment as its competitors strive forward in strategic success with one less opponent in the rear-view mirror. So you can't stop!

Figure 7.1 shows the situation when the performance assessment and strategic response development process has been completed and the library is prepared to implement and deliver the responses to the service environment:

- customer impact;
- value/cost-effectiveness;
- more access/less time;
- increased numbers of service options and resources.

Once these responses are implemented and affect the service environment, the environment begins to change. Needs are addressed or change over time; the demographics, economics, cultures and competitors are dynamic and evolve in the service environment. The needs of customers and stakeholders are changed (negatively or positively), and their expectations of how to address those needs are constantly in flux. The responses you introduced to the service environment have changed it (hopefully for the better), and it is now a different place with different needs. Your strategic responses will begin losing their effectiveness due to these changes, and there will be a need to review the impact and value of the responses to determine if their intended effectiveness and impact have materialized as planned or created negative impacts that must now be overcome. In short, you changed the service environment, so you will need to change the library's responses to the needs of that environment. So the library will need to continue developing new strategic responses following this process, to continue yielding strategic results and success for itself and the service environment.

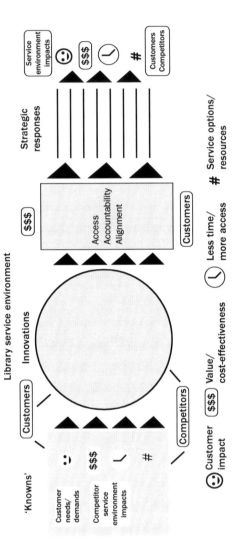

Figure 7.1 Strategic responses and service environment impacts

In order to continue to develop new strategic responses, the library will need to assess its performance, value creation, effectiveness and impacts in the service environment continually to identify its strategic assets, strengths and unmet needs. The processes by which the performance assessment information is obtained and used will also continue to develop and innovate, to allow the library the maximum ability to access the competitive information it needs to develop strategic responses.

The library must continue to know what aspects of its existing services provide impact, value and improved or expanded access, and to expand benefits and value to the customer in order to understand better the customers and stakeholders it serves and create strategic responses that are aligned to their changing needs. The library will continue to obtain and manage the 'knowns' because this component identifies what the library 'knows' or needs to 'know' about its service environment (i.e. customers, stakeholders and competitors), which is even more important than what it knows about itself. The library has to continue to ensure that the 'knowns' information is effectively obtained and managed in order to be successful in terms of identifying the ongoing information needed by the library and the sources of this information. Maintaining accurate information and data is essential to the overall success and effectiveness of the strategic response development model as well: if the library does not have accurate and complete information on its service environment and itself, it cannot continue to generate the most effective strategic decisions and responses that will create or maximize its impact and value for its service environment.

The customers (and even more importantly the non-customers) will continue to be a wealth of information for the competitive library seeking to develop or assess strategic responses. The library's customers will always share their insight about the library, its services and its desired and needed benefits with the library and its stakeholders. Ongoing analysis and understanding generated from the 'knowns' about the library and its service environment will continue to provide a mine of information to use in developing strategic responses and determining the effectiveness of or need for existing responses and services.

The competitive library will continue innovating its services and delivery of those services proactively to drive its competitive service environment. This process will keep the library connected to its customers, stakeholders and service environment even as the rest of the service environment continues its dynamic expansion and innovation. Continued innovation will keep customers interested and engaged with the library and help it to lobby and recruit new customers from the ranks of its competitors' customers. Continuous innovation also prevents the library and its staff from falling into complacent and reactive roles. By innovating services and delivery processes and capturing information and new customers from competitors, the library will provide itself with dynamic insights and perceptions of the service environment, ensuring that it has the widest insight into strategic opportunities and needs in this environment.

The library will continue to process the 'knowns' and the corresponding understanding from this information and data into innovations that generate potential strategic responses. These developing and strategic responses will continue to create potential positive impacts or values for the library's service environment and customers by effectively addressing the needs of that environment. Potential strategic responses will continue to be analyzed by the library to determine how to increase access to library services and benefits and create and demonstrate effective uses of library and service environment resources in implementing the possible responses.

Once potential strategic responses are developed, the competitive library will continue to analyze these responses in the evolving strategic development process. This will ensure that the responses align the library with its service environment in a positive or effective manner that generates positive impact for the library's environment. As effectively aligning the potential strategic responses is the most critical stage in the development process, continued analysis will ensure that a potential response effectively addresses need while generating the most value and impact for the library and its customers, stakeholders and service environment. The aligned strategic responses will continue through the development process, providing the library with options that increase the value and cost-effectiveness of its strategic responses while correspondingly aligning the responses with the needs of customers, stakeholders and the community within the service environment. Once a response is implemented, the competitive library will have to determine its performance and impacts and how the service environment has been impacted, and thus the process will continue.

You will notice that the word 'repeat' from the shampoo analogy has been replaced with the word 'continue'. Telling someone to repeat something implies that the process stops and then is restarted again and replayed the same exact way each time. Stopping the performance assessment and strategic response development process and attempting to repeat it later provides opportunities for distraction and creates inertia that has to be overcome to re-engage in the process. Also, repeating something implies that nothing changes; it is static in time and does not evolve or need to evolve in its surroundings.

Just as the library has to adapt to the service environment and its needs and continually be innovative in developing effective strategic responses, so must the process of developing these responses be continuous and adapt to be effective in generating the strategic responses for the competitive library.

The library itself is the primary party responsible for continuing the performance assessment and strategic response development process. As these processes are for the direct benefit of the library and performed by the library using its resources, it is imperative that the library should be the primary party responsible for and in control of these processes at all times. This does not, however, mean that the library is the only organization that should be involved in the processes. The five major stakeholders in the service environment – customers, stakeholders, competitors, non-library users and the library itself – must continue to be involved and welcomed participants in the processes, as they are all able to provide information that addresses questions exploring the multiple perceptions of services needed.

Warning! Hard work required!

Whether the library is beginning or continuing the performance assessment and strategic response development processes, competing in the library's service environment will continue to require hard work, dedication and commitment by the library's leaders and staff, and valuable resources if the processes are to be effective in increasing the library's strategic impact and competitive abilities.

There is nothing easy about being a competitive library in a dynamic service environment. A lot of work is required to implement and operate this or any other model of competitive or strategic response development. If you are successful in implementing strategic impact in the library's service environment, it not only makes a current positive impact but increases the expectations of the library and its next round of strategic responses. So the next iteration through the process only raises the bar of success a bit higher. This is the competitive world we live in, though. Our competitors operate and grow in this environment, and so must the library if it is to remain a vital strategic component of the service environment. Compete or not, our competitors are going to keep operating as if they are competing for survival against us, and we should be competing as well.

So if your library does not see it has competition, does not want to compete or take risks, be creative or innovative or work hard, or is not willing to commit effort and resources to implement a strategic process for the library to compete more effectively in its service environment, it should not begin the strategic response development or any other competitive response process. It will result in even more negative impact in the service environment to be overcome by the library, and waste resources and good staff.

Finally, please remember that competing is not a one-time-only event; it is an ongoing race of the fittest and if the library is not prepared to keep training and running in a competitive race, then save your resources and efforts. The library will need those resources and efforts to keep the competitors at bay as it slowly declines as a strategic component of the service environment.

It is up to the library what future it wants: slow decline or a hard-work, competitive thrill ride.

I wish you success in your endeavors, either way.

Appendix:
template forms for developing strategic responses

Library name/location:

Date __ / __ / __

Developing strategic responses: what are the 'knowns'?

This template is for recording the 'known' performance, value/impact and competitive information about the organization's service environment. The library should gather and record all its 'known' information on the library and its customers/stakeholders and competition in the appropriate places below. Everything recorded should be based on evidence only; not supposition or belief. Once completed, the 'knowns' template will serve as the starting point for the 'innovations' template.

Library service environment 'knowns' (continue on other pages if needed)

What is known about the...?	Service environment	Library	Customers/ stakeholders	Competitors
Culture				
Demographics				
Development plans				
Economic conditions				
Information sources				
Technologies				
Service needs				

Library name/location: Page __ of __

Date __ / __ / __

Developing strategic responses: what innovations are possible to create strategic responses?

> This template is for recording the possible innovations of library services, resources and technologies for improving value and impact in the organization's service environment. The library should brainstorm and record all its possible 'innovations' in the appropriate places. Everything recorded should be based on evidence only; not supposition or belief. Once completed, the 'innovations' template will serve as the starting point for the 'AAA' template.

Library service environment 'strategic responses' (continue on other pages if needed)

	Service environment	Library	Customers/ stakeholders
Given 'known' service needs (from 'knowns' template)			
Strategic responses: how can the library address the needs of each by...?			
Increasing/changing access to facilities?			
Increasing/changing access to resources?			
Increasing/changing access to technologies?			
Increasing/changing access to services?			
Decreasing customer wait times?			
Involving each in library planning?			

	Service environment	Library	Customers/ stakeholders
Given 'known' service needs (from 'knowns' template)			
Strategic responses: how can the library address the needs of each by...?			
Involving each in library performance assessment?			
Using innovations from competitors?			
Using innovations from service environment?			
Collaborating with competitors?			
Collaborating with other libraries?			

Library name/location:

Date __ / __ / __

Developing strategic responses: addressing access, accountability and alignment

This template is for recording how the proposed strategic responses from the 'innovations' template address the access, accountability and alignment (AAA) considerations of the library and its customers/stakeholders in order to maximize value and impact in the service environment. The library should compare the possible strategic responses to its needs and record the possible AAA strategic considerations in the appropriate places. Once completed, the 'AAA' template will serve as the starting point for the 'strategic responses' template.

Library service environment 'impact and value' (continue on other pages if needed)

	Service environment	Library	Customers/ stakeholders
Given the possible 'innovations' to generate strategic responses (from 'innovations' template):	1. 2. 3. 4. 5.	1. 2. 3. 4. 5.	1. 2. 3. 4. 5.
How can each strategic response improve the library's ability to demonstrate...?			
Access (improved or wider scope of access to library services and resources by customers, stakeholders and service environment)	1. 2. 3. 4. 5.	1. 2. 3. 4. 5.	1. 2. 3. 4. 5.

	Service environment	Library	Customers/ stakeholders
How can each strategic response improve the library's ability to demonstrate...?			
Accountability (improved accountability of library use of resources in meeting service environment needs, creating greater service value or impact for library customers, stakeholders and service environment)	1. 2. 3. 4. 5.	1. 2. 3. 4. 5.	1. 2. 3. 4. 5.
Alignment (improved connections between library services provided and services needed by service environment, improved or wider scope of participation in library operations and services, improved ability to communicate library performance and value to service environment)	1. 2. 3. 4. 5.	1. 2. 3. 4. 5.	1. 2. 3. 4. 5.

Library name/location: Page __ of __

Date __ / __ / __

Developing strategic responses: strategic response compilation

> This template is for recording how the best strategic responses from the 'AAA' template will address the needs of the service environment and identifying the best strategic options that improve the library's ability to demonstrate access, accountability and alignment to customers, stakeholders and the service environment. The library can then use the compilation of strategic information to develop priorities, plans of action, activities' lists and resource allocations using its own strategic planning style.

Library service environment (continue on other pages if needed)

Given the potential strategic responses (from AAA template)	Strategic needs addressed	Strategic innovations required	Strategic value/ impacts
1.			
2.			
3.			
4.			
5.			

What does the library need to accomplish these potential strategic responses?			
The library needs...	From service environment	From library	From customers/ stakeholders/ competitors
Information			
Information sources			
Performance assessment information			
Administrative/staff time			

What does the library need to accomplish these potential strategic responses?			
The library needs...	From service environment	From library	From customers/ stakeholders/ competitors
Staff knowledge/skills/ abilities			
Financial resources			
Collaborators			
Participation			
Marketing/PR			
Stop doing			
Policy/procedural changes			
Technologies			

References

Ammons, David N. (2000) *Municipal Benchmarks: Assessing Local Performance and Establishing Community Standards*. Thousand Oaks, CA: Sage Publications.

DeProspo, Ernest R., Altman, Ellen and Beasley, Kenneth E. (1973) *Performance Measures for Public Libraries*. Chicago: PLA.

Halachmi, Arie and Bouckaert, Geert (eds) (1996) *Organizational Performance and Measurement in the Public Sector: Toward Service, Effort, and Accomplishment Reporting*. Westport, CT: Quorum Books.

Hatry, Harry P., Blair, Louise, Fisk, Donald M., Greiner, John H., Hall, John R. and Schaenman, Philip S. (1979) *Efficiency Measurement for Local Government Services – Some Initial Suggestions*. Washington, DC: Urban Institute.

Hernon, Peter and Altman, Ellen (1998) *Assessing Service Quality: Satisfying the Expectations of Library Customers*. Chicago: American Library Association.

Institute for Museum and Library Services (2000) *Perspectives on Outcome Based Evaluation for Libraries and Museums*. Washington, DC: IMLS.

International Federation of Library Associations (1986) *Guidelines for Public Libraries*. Munich: Saur/IFLA.

Kanter, R.M. and Summers, V.D. (1987) 'Doing well while doing good: dilemmas of performance measurement in non-profit organizations and the need for a multiple constituency approach', in Walter W. Powell (ed.)

The Nonprofit Sector: A Research Handbook. New Haven: Yale University Press, pp. 154–66.

Kaplan, Robert S. (2001) 'Strategic performance measurement and management in nonprofit organizations', *Nonprofit Management and Leadership*, 11(3): 353–70.

Kraft, D.H. and Boyce, Bert R. (1991) *Operations Research for Libraries and Information Agencies: Techniques for the Evaluation of Management Decision Alternatives*. San Diego, CA: Academic Press.

Lakos, Amos (1999) 'The missing ingredient – culture of assessment in libraries', *Performance Measurement and Metrics*, 1(1): 3–7.

Lancaster, F.W. (1977) *The Measurement and Evaluation of Library Services*. Washington, DC: Information Resources Press.

Lawes, A. (1993) 'The benefits of quality management to the library and information profession', *Special Libraries*, 84(3): 142–6.

Letts, Christine, Ryan, William and Grossman, Allen (1999) *High Performance Nonprofit Organizations: Managing Upstream for Greater Impact*. New York: John Wiley & Sons.

Liddle, Mark (1999) 'Best value – the impact on libraries: practical steps in demonstrating best value', *Library Management*, 20(4): 206–14.

Lubans, J.J. and Chapman, Edward A. (1975) *Reader in Library Systems Analysis*, Reader Series in Library and Information Science. Englewood, CO: Microcard Edition Books.

Lynch, M.J. (1990) 'Measurement of library output: how is it related to research', in C.C. Curran and F.W. Summers (eds) *Library Performance, Accountability, and Responsiveness: Essays in Honor of Ernest R. DeProspo*. Norwood, NJ: Ablex Publishing, pp. 1–8.

Metcalfe, Henry (1885) *The Cost of Manufactures and the Administration of Workshops Public and Private.* New York: John Wiley & Sons.

Owens, Robert ([1815] 1977) *Observations on the Effect of the Manufacturing System*, 2nd edn. Chicago: University of Chicago Press.

Risher, Howard and Fay, Charles (eds) (1995) *The Performance Imperative: Strategies for Enhancing Workforce Effectiveness.* San Francisco: Jossey-Bass Publishers.

Shafritz, Jay M. and Ott, J. Stephen (eds) (1997) *Classics of Public Administration*, 4th edn. Fort Worth, TX: Harcourt Brace College Publishers.

Smith, Adam (1776) *An Inquiry Into the Nature and Causes of the Wealth of Nations.* London: R.&A. Taylor.

Taylor, Frederick (1911) *The Principles of Scientific Management.* New York: Harper Brothers.

Van House, Nancy A., Lynch, Mary Jo, McClure, Charles R., Zweizig, Douglas L. and Rodger, Eleanor Jo (1987) *Output Measures for Public Libraries: A Manual of Standardized Procedures*, 2nd edn. Chicago: American Library Association.

Wedgeworth, R. (ed.) (1993) *World Encyclopedia of Library and Information Science*, 3rd edn. Chicago: American Library Association.

White, Larry Nash (2002) 'Does counting count? An evaluative study of the perceptions and uses of performance measurement in Florida public libraries', dissertation, Florida State University, Tallahassee, Florida.

Bibliography

Altman, Ellen (1990) 'Reflections on performance measures fifteen years later', in C.C. Curran and F. William Summers (eds) *Library Performance, Accountability, and Responsiveness: Essays in Honor of Ernest R. DeProspo*. Norwood, NJ: Ablex Publishing, pp. 9–16.

American Library Association (1980) *Library Effectiveness: A State of the Art*. New York: American Library Association.

Babbie, Earl (1998) *The Practice of Social Research*, 8th edn. Belmont, CA: Wadsworth Publishing.

Bassett, Glenn (1993) *The Evolution and Future of High Performance Management Systems*. Westport, CT: Quorum Books.

Belasen, Alan T. (1999) *Leading the Learning Organization: Communication and Competencies for Managing Change*. Albany, NY: State University of New York Press.

Bell, C.R. (1994) *Customers As Partners: Building Relationships That Last*. San Francisco: Berrett-Koehler Publishers.

Benton Foundation (1996) *Americans Chart a Future for Public Libraries*. Washington, DC: W.W. Kellogg Foundation.

Bertot, John Carlo, McClure, Charles R. and Ryan, Joe (2001) *Statistics and Performance Measures for Public Library Networked Services*. Chicago: American Library Association.

Best, David P. (ed.) (1996) *The Fourth Resource: Information and Its Management*. Aldershot: ASLIB Gower.

Bjornlund, Lydia (1999) *Beyond Data: Current Uses of Comparative Performance Measurement in Local Government*. Washington, DC: International City/County Management Association.

Black, S.A. and Porter, Leslie (1996) 'Identification of the critical factors of TQM', *Decision Sciences*, 27(1): 1–21.

Blagden, John and Harrington, John (1990) *How Good Is Your Library? A Review of Approaches to the Evaluation of Library and Information Services*. London: ASLIB.

Blank, Joseph L.T. (ed.) (2000) *Public Provision and Performance: Contributions from Efficiency and Productivity Measurement*. Amsterdam: Elsevier.

Boekhorst, Peter (1995) 'Measuring quality: the IFLA guidelines for performance measurement in academic libraries', *IFLA Journal*, 21(4): 278–81.

Bogan, C. and English, Michael J. (1994) *Benchmarking for Best Practices: Winning Through Innovative Adoption*. New York: McGraw-Hill.

Boisse, J.A. (1996) 'Adjusting the horizontal hold: flattening the organization', *Library Administrative & Management*, 10(2): 77–81.

Bourn, J. (1995) *Public Sector Management. International Library of Management, Vol. 2*. Vermont: Dartmouth Publishing.

Boyce, Bert R., Meadow, Charles T. and Craft, Donald H. (1994) *Measurement in Information Science*. San Diego, CA: Academic Press.

Brewer, J. (1995) 'Service management: how to plan for it rather than hope for it', *Library Administration and Management*, 9(4): 207–10.

Brimson, J.A. (1994) *Activity Based Management: For Service Industries, Government Entities, and Nonprofit Organizations*. New York: John Wiley & Sons.

Brocka, B. and Brocka, M. Suzanne (1992) *Quality Management: Implementing the Best Ideas of the Masters*. Homewood, IL: Business One Irwin.

Brockman, J.R. (1992) 'Just another management fad? The implications of TQM for library and information services', *ASLIB Proceedings*, 44(7/8): 283–8.

Brockman, John (ed.) (1997) *Quality Management and Benchmarking in the Information Sector*. London: Bowker-Saur.

Brooking, Annie (1999) *Corporate Memory: Strategies for Knowledge Management*. London: Thomson International Business Press.

Brooks, Terrance Alan (1981) *An Analysis of Library-output Statistics*. Austin, TX: University of Texas.

Brophy, Peter and Coulling, Kate (1996) *Quality Management for Information and Library Managers*. London: ASLIB Gower.

Brown, M.G. (1996) *Keeping Score: Using the Right Metrics to Drive World-class Performance*. New York: Quality Resources.

Campbell, J.D. (1996) 'Building an effectiveness pyramid for leading successful organizational transformation', *Library Administration & Management*, 10(2): 82–6.

Carr, D.K. and Johansson, Henry J. (1995) *Best Practices in Reengineering: What Works and What Doesn't in the Reengineering Process*. New York: McGraw-Hill.

Chen, C. (1978) *Quantitative Measurement and Dynamic Library Service*. Phoenix, AZ: Oryx Press.

Childers, Thomas and Van House, Nancy A. (1989) *The Public Library Effectiveness Study: Final Report*. Washington, DC: US Department of Education.

Childers, Thomas and Van House, Nancy A. (1993) *What's Good? Describing Your Public Library's Effectiveness.* Chicago: American Library Association.

Ciborra, Claudio U., Braa, Kristin, Cordella, Antonio and Dahlbom, Bo (2000) *From Control to Drift: The Dynamics of Corporate Information Infrastructures.* Oxford: Oxford University Press.

Clark, Alan and Dawson, Ruth (1999) *Evaluation Research: An Introduction to Principles, Methods, and Practice.* London: Sage Publications.

Collier, D.A. (1993) *The Service/Quality Solution: Using Service Management to Gain Competitive Advantage.* Milwaukee, WI: ASQC Quality Press.

Curran, C. and Clark, Phillip M. (1989) 'Implications of tying state aid to performance measures', *Public Libraries,* 28(6): 348–54.

Davis, F.W. and Manrodt, Karl B. (1996) *Customer-responsive Management: The Flexible Advantage.* Cambridge, MA: Blackwell.

Dixon, Nancy M. (1999) *Common Knowledge: How Companies Thrive by Sharing What They Know.* Boston, MA: Harvard Business School Press.

Drucker, P.F. (1980) *Managing in Turbulent Times.* New York: Harper and Row.

Earl, Michael J. (ed.) (1995) *Information Management: The Organizational Dimension.* New York: Oxford University Press.

Edosomwan, J.A. (1987) 'Integrating productivity and quality management', in *Industrial Engineering, Vol. 14.* New York: Marcel Dekker.

Evans, J., Anderson, D.R., Sweeney, D.J. and Williams, T.A. (1990) *Applied Production and Operations Management.* St Paul, MN: West Publishing.

Finch, B.J. and Luebbe, Richard L. (1995) *Operations Management: Competing in a Changing Environment.* Orlando, FL: Dryden Press.

Fisher, W. (1995) 'Does TQM really help anyone?', *Library Acquisitions: Practice and Theory*, 19(1): 49–52.

Gale, B.T. (1993) *Managing Customer Value: Creating Quality and Service that Customers Can See.* New York: Free Press.

Garrod, P. and Kinnell, Margaret (1996) 'Performance measurement, benchmarking, and the UK library and information services sector', *Libri*, 46(3): 141–8.

Glazier, Jack D. and Powell, Ronald R. (eds) (1992) *Qualitative Research in Information Management.* Englewood, CO: Libraries Unlimited.

Goleski, E. (1995) 'Learning to say, "Yes": a customer service program for library staff', *Library Administration & Management*, 9(4): 211–15.

Gray, Sandra Trice (1997) *Evaluation with Power: A New Approach to Organizational Effectiveness, Empowerment, and Excellence.* San Francisco: Jossey-Bass Publishers.

Haavind, R. (1991) *The Road to the Baldridge Award: Quest for Total Quality.* Stoneham, MA: Butterworth-Heinemann.

Harris, M. (1991) 'The customer survey in performance measurement', *British Journal of Academic Librarianship*, 6(1): 1–27.

Hays, R.D. (1996) *Internal Service Excellence: A Manager's Guide to Building World Class Internal Service Unit Performance.* Sarasota, FL: Summit Executive Press.

Hernon, Peter (1992) 'Library and information science research: not an island unto itself', *Library & Information Science Research*, 14(1/3): 1–3.

Hernon, Peter (1996) 'Service quality in libraries and treating customers as customers and non-customers as lost or never-gained customers', *Journal of Academic Librarianship*, 22(3): 171–2.

Hernon, Peter and Altman, Ellen (1996) *Service Quality in Academic Libraries*. Chicago: American Library Association.

Hernon, Peter and McClure, Charles R. (1990) *Evaluation and Decision Making*. Norwood, NJ: Ablex Publishing.

Hernon, Peter and Whitman, John R. (2001) *Delivering Satisfaction and Service Quality: A Customer-based Approach for Libraries*. Chicago: American Library Association.

Hershfield, Allan F. and Boone, Morell D. (1972) *Approaches to Measuring Library Effectiveness: A Symposium*. Syracuse, NY: Syracuse University Press.

Heskett, J.L. (1990) *Service Breakthroughs: Changing the Rules of the Game*. New York: Free Press.

Hunt, V.D. (1993) *Managing for Quality: Integrating Quality and Business Strategy*. Homewood, IL: Business One Irwin.

Jensen, Bill (2000) *Simplicity: The New Competitive Advantage in a World of More, Better, Faster*. New York: Perseus Publishing.

Johnson, R.S. (1993) *TQM: Leadership for the Quality Transformation*. Milwaukee, WI: ASQC Quality Press.

Jossey-Bass (1994) *The Jossey-Bass Handbook of Nonprofit Leadership and Management*. San Francisco: Jossey-Bass Publishers.

Kaplan, Robert S. and Norton, David P. (1996) *The Balanced Scorecard: Translating Strategy into Action*. Boston, MA: Harvard Business School Press.

Kearney, Richard C. and Berman, Evan M. (1999) *Public Sector Performance: Management, Motivation, and Measurement*. Boulder, CO: Westview Press.

Kemp, R.L. (1995) 'The creative management of library services', *Public Libraries*, 34(4): 212–15.

Keyes, J. (1992) *Infotrends: The Competitive Use of Information*. New York: McGraw-Hill.

Lancaster, F.W. (1988) *If You Want to Evaluate Your Library...* Champaign, IL: University of Illinois.

Lawler, E.E. II (1980) *Organizational Assessment: Perspectives on the Measurement of Organizational Behavior and the Quality of Work Life*. New York: John Wiley & Sons.

Lee, S. and Clack, Mary Elizabeth (1996) 'Continued organizational transformation: the Harvard College Library's experience', *Library Administration & Management*, 10(2): 98–104.

Leimkuhler, F.F. (1977) 'Operations research and systems analysis', in F.W. Lancaster (ed.) *Evaluation and Scientific Management of Libraries and Information Centers*. Bristol: Noordhoff International, pp. 131–64.

Liu, Kecheng, Clarke, Rodney J., Andersen, Peter Bogh and Stamper, Ronald K. (eds) (2000) *Information, Organization, and Technology: Studies in Organizational Semiotics*. Norwell, MA: Kluwer Academic Publishers.

Losee, R.M. and Worley, Karen A. (1993) *Research and Evaluation for Information Professionals*. San Diego, CA: Academic Press.

Lynch, B.P. (1985) *Management Strategies for Libraries: A Basic Reader*. New York: Neal-Schuman Publishers.

McClelland, S.B. (1995) *Organizational Needs Assessments: Design, Facilitation, and Analysis*. Westport, CT: Quorum Books.

McClure, Charles R. (1990) 'Integrating performance measures into the planning process: moving toward decision support systems', in C.C. Curran and F. William Summers (eds) *Library Performance, Accountability, and Responsiveness: Essays in Honor of Ernest R. DeProspo*. Norwood, NJ: Ablex Publishing, pp. 17–32.

McClure, Charles R. and Hernon, Peter (eds) (1990) *Library and Information Science Research: Perspectives and Strategies for Improvement*. Norwood, NJ: Ablex Publishing.

McGee, James V., Prusak, Laurence and Pyburn, Philip J. (1993) *Managing Information Strategically*. New York: John Wiley & Sons.

Miles, Matthew B. and Huberman, A. Michael (1984) *Qualitative Data Analysis: A Sourcebook of New Methods*. Beverly Hills, CA: Sage Publications.

Miller, W.C. (1993) *Quantum Quality: Quality Improvement Through Innovation, Learning, and Creativity*. White Plains, NY: Quality Resources.

Milner, Eileen M. (2000) *Managing Information and Knowledge in the Public Sector*. London: Routledge.

Moore, N. (1989) *Measuring the Performance of Public Libraries*. New York: UNESCO.

Moorman, J.A. (1997) 'Standards for public libraries: a study in quantitative measures of library performance as found in state public library documents', *Public Libraries*, 36(1): 32–9.

Noble, P. and Ward, Patricia Layzell (1976) 'Performance measures and criteria for libraries', in *Public Library Occasional Papers, Vol. 3*. Brighton: Orchard & Ind.

Obloj, Krzysatof, Cushman, Donald P. and Kozminskis, Andrzej (1994) *Winning: Continuous Improvement Theory in High-performance Organizations*. Albany, NY: State University of New York.

Oldham, C. (1977) 'An examination of cost/benefit approaches to the evaluation of library and information services', in F.W. Lancaster (ed.) *Evaluation and Scientific Management of Libraries and Information Centers*. Bristol: Noordhoff International, pp. 165–84.

O'Neil, Rosanna M. and Osif, Bonnie Anne (1993) 'A total look at TQM: a TQM perspective from the literature of business, industry, higher education, and librarianship', *Library Administration & Management*, 7(4): 244–54.

Ormes, S. (1996) 'Access is limited in quantity and quality', *Library Association Record*, 98(1): 68.

Park, Mary Woodfill (1998) *InfoThink: Practical Strategies for Using Information in Business*. Lanham, MD: Scarecrow Press.

Patton, Michael Quinn (1980) *Qualitative Evaluation Methods*. Beverly Hills, CA: Sage Publications.

Peters, B. Guy and Pierre, Jon (2001) *Politicians, Bureaucrats, and Administrative Reform*. London: Routledge.

Pfeffer, Jeffrey and Sutton, Robert L. (1999) *The Knowing-Doing Gap: How Smart Companies Turn Knowledge into Action*. Boston, MA: Harvard Business School Press.

Poll, Roswitha (1991) 'Problems of performance evaluation in academic libraries', *INSPEL*, 25(1): 25–36.

Pritchard, R.D. (1990) *Measuring and Improving Organizational Productivity: A Practical Guide*. New York: Praeger.

Pritchard, R.D. (1995) *Productivity Measurement and Improvement: Organizational Case Studies*. Westport, CT: Praeger.

Prusak, Lawrence (ed.) (1997) *Knowledge in Organizations*. Boston, MA: Butterworth-Heinemann.

Robbins, Jane (ed.) (1988) *Rethinking the Library in the Information Age*. Washington, DC: US Department of Education.

Robbins, Jane and Zweizig, Douglas (1988) *Are We There Yet? Evaluating Library Collections, Reference Services,*

Programs, and Personnel. Madison, WI: University of Wisconsin-Madison.

Rust, R.T. and Oliver, Richard L. (eds) (1994) *Service Quality: New Directions in Theory and Practice.* Thousand Oaks, CA: Sage Publications.

St Clair, G. (1996) 'Total quality management in information services', in *Information Services Management, Vol. 6.* London: Bowker-Saur.

Schement, Jorge Reina (1996) 'A 21st century strategy for librarians', *Library Journal,* 121(8): 34–6.

Scriven, Michael (1991) *Evaluation Thesaurus,* 4th edn. Thousand Oaks, CA: Sage Publications.

Shaffer, K.R. (1972) *The Experience of Management.* Metuchen, NJ: Scarecrow Press.

Smith, Mark (1996) *Collecting and Using Public Library Statistics.* New York: Neal-Schuman Publishers.

Snyder, Herbert (1997) 'Protecting our assets: internal control principles in libraries', *Library Administration and Management,* 11(1): 42–6.

Special Libraries Association (1998) *Knowledge Management: A New Competitive Asset.* Washington, DC: Special Libraries Association.

Suchman, Edward Allen (1967) *Evaluation Research: Principles and Practice in Public Service and Social Action Programs.* New York: Sage Foundation.

Tague-Sutcliffe, Jean (1996) *Measuring Information: An Information Services Perspective.* San Diego, CA: Academic Press.

Thompson, A.A. and Strickland, A.J. III (1984) *Strategic Management: Concepts and Cases.* Plano, TX: Business Publications.

Thompson, J. (1991) *Redirection in Academic Library Management.* London: Library Association Publishing.

Tiefel, V. (1989) 'Output or performance measures: the making of a manual', *C&RL News*, June: 475–8.

Travica, Bob (1998) *New Organizational Designs: Information Aspects*. Stamford, CT: Ablex Publishing.

Tushman, M.L. and Anderson, Philip (1997) *Managing Strategic Innovation and Change*. Oxford: Oxford University Press.

United Way of America (1995–2002) 'Outcome measurement resource network'; available at: *www/unitedway.org/outcomes/* (accessed: 18 July 2007).

Wallace, Danny P. and Van Fleet, Connie (2001) *Library Evaluation: A Casebook and Can-do Guide*. Englewood, CO: Libraries Unlimited.

Wilson, Paul F. and Pearson, Richard D. (1995) *Performance-based Assessments: External, Internal, and Self-assessment Tools for Total Quality Management*. Milwaukee, WI: ASQC Quality Press.

Withers, F.N. (1974) *Standards for Library Service: An International Survey*. Paris: UNESCO.

Zweizig, Douglas and Rodgers, Eleanor Jo (1982) *Output Measures for Public Libraries: A Manual of Standardized Procedures*. Chicago: American Library Association.

Zweizig, Douglas, Johnson, Debra Wilcox, Robbins, Jane and Besant, Michele (1994) *Tell It! Evaluation Sourcebook and Training Manual*. Madison, WI: University of Wisconsin.

Index

AAA (access, accountability, alignment), 63, 92, 110, 112, 114

accountability, 4–5, 7, 11–12, 17–18, 25, 27, 87, 90–3, 95, 97, 100, 112–13

American Library Association (ALA), 8

assessment, 1

balanced score card (BSC), 9–10

Baldridge, Malcolm, 10

benchmarking, 10

best value, 20

Brandeis, Louis, 3

capacity, 10

Chartered Institute of Library and Information Professionals (CILIP), 8

Chevrolet, 88

Coca-Cola, 89

community capital, 10

competition, 4, 100, 109

  business, 6

  increasing, 4, 12

  library, 18, 39–55, 107

  for service, 22, 28, 55, 59, 61

competitors, 4, 26–8, 30, 39–50, 52–3, 55, 58–66, 79–81, 83, 86–7, 91, 94–5, 97–8, 101–4, 106–7, 109, 111, 114–15

competitive intelligence, 10, 60

cost avoidance, 10

customer/stakeholder:

  inclusion in library assessment, 8, 36–7, 56, 127

  in service environment, 59, 66

customer capital, 10

demographics, 10

evaluation, 12, 34

  macro-evaluation, 12

  micro-evaluation, 12

expert valuation, 10

Facebook, 40

FedEx, 50–2

financial capital, 10

Google, 39

governmental agencies/ organizations, 5, 20, 47–8, 83

  as competitors to libraries, 39, 41–2, 44

human capital, 10

Industrial Revolution, 1

Institute for Museum and Library Services (IMLS), 16

intellectual capital, 10